The Future of Marriage

ISSUES

Volume 40

Editor

Craig Donnellan

Independence
Educational Publishers
Cambridge

First published by Independence
PO Box 295
Cambridge CB1 3XP
England

British Library Cataloguing in Publication Data
The Future of Marriage – (Issues Series)
I. Donnellan, Craig II. Series
306.8'1

ISBN 1 86168 217 4

Printed in Great Britain
MWL Print Group Ltd

Typeset by
Claire Boyd

Cover
The illustration on the front cover is by
Pumpkin House.

CONTENTS

Introduction

The Future of Marriage is the fortieth volume in the **Issues** series. The aim of this series is to offer up-to-date information about important issues in our world.

The Future of Marriage examines the issues of cohabitation and marriage, separation and divorce.

The information comes from a wide variety of sources and includes:
Government reports and statistics
Newspaper reports and features
Magazine articles and surveys
Literature from lobby groups
and charitable organisations.

It is hoped that, as you read about the many aspects of the issues explored in this book, you will critically evaluate the information presented. It is important that you decide whether you are being presented with facts or opinions. Does the writer give a biased or an unbiased report? If an opinion is being expressed, do you agree with the writer?

The Future of Marriage offers a useful starting-point for those who need convenient access to information about the many issues involved. However, it is only a starting-point. At the back of the book is a list of organisations which you may want to contact for further information.

*****

The family today

An at-a-glance guide

During the 20th century, improved health and living standards meant that people lived longer, more active lives along with having more leisure time and the means to enjoy it. Families became smaller as the birth rate fell and women married, then had children, at a later age. More women remained childless. The number of households increased. More people lived alone and more single parents established their own household. More couples lived together, or divorced and remarried. The part that the family plays in our everyday lives is also changing. As we move into the 21st century, most people will spend a much smaller part of their active life bringing up dependent children. Only one-fifth of households are made up of a married couple with dependent children.[14]

Family life

21st-century parents spend an average of about an hour and a half a day with their children – helping with homework, swimming, talking, sorting out problems or visiting museums and theme parks. This compares with an average of half an hour a day in the 1970s.[7]

When families in the UK were asked to make their family trees, they discovered tens and hundreds of connections to cousins or step-relatives and their families – people whom they had not spoken to or kept in touch with for many years.[1]

But when families in the USA were asked what makes a family, the majority answered that doing things together was most important.[6]

So although the feeling of belonging to a family is the most important thing in life for approximately three in four people in the UK today[15] day-to-day contact with family is quite different.

More people include close friends in the wider circle of family often providing emotional support on a day-to-day basis.[1, 8]

There are more four- and five-generation families today than there were one hundred years ago.[1]

Eleven per cent of changes in households including older people happen when younger-generation adults move back into the family home.[17]

At the beginning of the 21st century, around 1 in 3 families have a home computer,[2] more than 13 million people have access to the Internet[3] and half the population has a mobile phone.[1]

New technology makes it easier for family members to keep in touch across distances.

Who is the family today?

There are just over 16 million families and 12 million children in the UK today.[14]

In 1998, 3 in 4 families were two-parent families.[14]

In 2000 three-fifths of all households were headed by a couple.[16]

In 1999 there were just over a quarter of a million (293,000) marriages in the UK: one of the lowest annual figures recorded in the 20th century.[16]

In 1999 just over 40 per cent of weddings were remarriages for one or both partners. The number of second or third marriages trebled at the end of the last century.[16]

There are over one and a half million one-parent families in the UK today.[11]

In 1999 the total ethnic minority population in the UK was 3,702,000 living in 1,308,000 households.[2]

By the end of the 20th century just over 50,000 children were looked after in residential care.[13]

In 1999 between 4,000 and 6,000 children were adopted in the UK and between 2,400 and 5,000 were awaiting adoption.[14]

Over a third of children in the UK were living in poverty in 1999 compared to only one in ten in 1979. Over half (62 per cent) of lone parents live in poverty. 30 per cent of children live in a family without a full-time worker.[5]

Marriage and relationships today

Just over half the adult population of Great Britain are married.[4]

Nine out of ten couples living with their children are married.[14]

In 1996, there were 1.6 million cohabiting couples in England and Wales – two-thirds were single and a quarter divorced.[14]

In 1998, more than one in ten adults had cohabited in a relationship that did not lead to marriage and for people aged 25 to 29, the figure rose to one in four.[14]

In 1999, 159,000 divorces were granted in the United Kingdom.[16]

Although the divorce rate peaked in 1993, two in five marriages will still ultimately end in divorce.[18]

Over a quarter of divorces in 1997 were granted to people married for between five and ten years.[2]

Over half (60 per cent) of divorces in 1997 were to couples where the woman was under 25 when they first married.[2]

Over half (60 per cent) of divorces in 1997 were to couples with children.[2]

In 1996, over two-thirds (70 per cent) of divorces were granted to couples who had both married for the first time.[2]

In 1999 two-fifths of all marriages were of couples where at least one of the partners had been married before.[16]

There were over 10,000 more divorces granted in the early 1990s than by the end of the 20th century.[2]

The average length of marriages in England and Wales was 24 years in 1994, compared to 37 years in 1980.[12]

The average length of a first-time-round cohabiting relationship was between three and four years in the 1970s and 1980s.[12]

1.3 per cent of couples are from different ethnic backgrounds.[13]

Lone parents

At the end of the 20th century, nearly a quarter of children lived in a single-parent family – a total of around 3 million children.[10]

The proportion of lone-parent households with dependent children more than trebled in the second half of the 20th century to 7 per cent of all households in 1999.[14]

Almost one in five dependent children live in lone-mother families.[16]

Lone-father families accounted for 2 per cent of all families with dependent children in 2000.[16]

One-parent families are now a stage in the life cycle lasting about five years.[11]

One in seven lone mothers has never married or lived with the father of her child.[14]

Stepfamilies

Nine out of ten stepfamilies with dependent children are made up of a couple living with at least some children from the woman's previous relationship.[14]

According to the *General Household Survey*, in 1999, 6 per cent of all families with dependent children were stepfamilies.[16]

30 per cent of unmarried women (separated, divorced or widowed) with dependent children were cohabiting in 1997.[14]

Finding out more about the family

This article summarises the key facts about the family in the UK today in an 'at a glance' format. Most of the information comes from government sources and research reports commissioned by industry, charities or think tanks. These organisations commission studies that paint a picture of the family today in Britain so that they can plan policy and services as well as predict future trends. Sometimes researchers have to keep pace with changes that are happening very quickly. Sometimes trends are known to exist but there is no hard evidence. For example, there is little information about the numbers of children growing up in 'unofficial' stepfamilies (where neither partner is remarried or cohabiting full-time) or in part-time stepfamilies (where the children spend time with both parents in turn), in gay families or in families where parents are each from a different religion or culture.

References

1 M. Anderson, J. Tunaley, J. Walker *Relatively Speaking: Communication in Families*, Newcastle Centre for Family Studies, University of Newcastle upon Tyne for The BT Forum, 2000

2 *Annual Abstract of Statistics 2000*, Office for National Statistics (ONS)

3 Tony Blair, The Information Society, *The Guardian* 25.10.99

4 *Britain 2000, The Official Yearbook of the United Kingdom* (ONS)

5 Child Poverty Action Group, *Poverty Briefing*, 2000

6 J. English-Lueck, unpublished research, San Jose University, USA, reported in *The Guardian*, 17 May 2000

7 Jonathan Gershuny, ISER, University of Essex with the Future Foundation for Abbey National, 2000

8 Christina Hardyment, *The Future of the Family* Phoenix, 1998

9 Haskey, J., The proportion of married couples who divorce, *Population Trends 83*

10 Living in Britain: Results from the 1998 *General Household Survey*, Office for National Statistics Social Survey Division, 2000

11 National Council for One-Parent Families, *One-Parent Families Today – The Facts*, 1999

12 *Parliamentary Monitor*, May 2000

13 *Social Focus on Ethnic Minorities*, Office for National Statistics, 1998

14 *Social Trends 30*, Office for National Statistics, The Stationery Office, 2000

15 Helen Wilkinson (ed.), *Family Business*, Demos Collection: issue 15, 2000

16 *Social Trends 31*, Office for National Statistics, The Stationery Office 2001

17 *Population Trends 105*, Office for National Statistics, The Stationery Office 2001

18 *One-Parent Families Today*, National Council for One-Parent Families, 2001

• The above information is from the National Family and Parenting Institute (NFPI). See page 41 for their address details.

Changing trends in family life

Information from CARE – Christian Action Research and Education

'Family life is the foundation on which our communities, our society and our country are built.' Yet in the UK there are increasingly divergent views on what actually constitutes 'the family', and there is now widespread acceptance of different forms of family life: cohabitation, lone parenthood, same-sex partnerships as well as heterosexual marriage. It is estimated that the total adult population will rise by 10% between 1996 and 2021, yet the total number of single and divorced people will both increase by around 50%. In comparison, the married population will fall by 10%. As a result, married people will become a minority of the adult population within the next 10 years.

The rapid structural changes in family life have been caused by a number of factors, some positive and some negative. These include:

- the declining influence of the Church and 'traditional' religion
- increasing individualism
- changing attitudes to marriage and its commitment
- the consequences (often unintended) of divorce reforms
- the wide availability of reliable contraception and abortion
- the liberalisation of sexual and moral values and attitudes
- changes in the roles of women
- economic trends in female and male employment
- increased mobility and the disintegration of community life.

'People still want companionship, friendship, security, love, children. A stable family and a good job are the two most important things in life.'

Marriage

In 2000, 71% of all dependent children in the UK were in families headed by a married couple, compared to 10% of dependent children in families headed by a cohabiting couple. Importantly, 70% of children born within marriage will live their entire childhood with both natural parents.

The robustness of marriage is illustrated by statistics that reveal only 14% of people agree that marriage is out of date and 82% of young people between 16 and 17 years still expect to marry.

However, as has been widely documented and reported, the number of married couples is steadily falling, partly due to couples waiting longer before they marry and partly due to continually rising divorce rates. In 1999 there were 264,000 marriages, a drop of 1.4% from 1998, and 24% less than 1989. 59% of these were first marriages for both partners. The mean age at first marriage in 1999 was 28 years for women and 30 years for men. In 1981, just 18 years earlier, the average ages were 22 and 24 years respectively.

There has been a steady shift away from religious marriage ceremonies to civil over the past 30 years. In 1999, 62% of marriages were civil marriage ceremonies, compared to 41% in 1971.

The importance of marriage to children, adults and society is now well documented. Marriage is associated with measurable improvements in labour market participation, health, well-being and life-expectancy for adults: 'There is an intimate link between marital status and personal well-being. Numerous investigations, beginning decades ago attest that married people live longer and generally are more emotionally and physically healthy than the unmarried.' Marriage is also important for children – children who are raised outside 'traditional' married families suffer higher rates of mortality, are at higher risk of physical abuse, crime and delinquency, are more likely to be taken into care, to become homeless, to become teenage parents and in turn to experience the breakdown of their own relationships. Marriage is the most effective safeguard for women and children from violence, poverty and neglect.

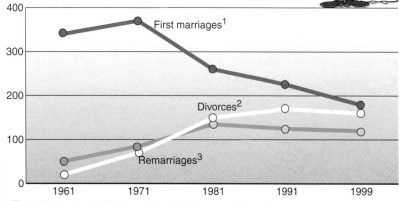

Marriages and divorces in the UK

The pattern of partnership formation has changed since the mid-1970s. Although the majority of men and women still get married, the proportion who marry has been declining and the proportions who cohabit or live outside a relationship have increased.

First marriages[1]

Divorces[2]

Remarriages[3]

1 For both partners, 2 Includes annulments, 3 For one or both partners.
Source: Office for National Statistics; General Register for Scotland; Northern Ireland Statistics and Research Agency

Cohabitation

There has been a great rise in the popularity of living together before, or instead of, getting married. In the UK, 34% of couples under 30 are cohabiting: 'Cohabitation is the most common form of first partnership for young adults today.'

However, 'Cohabitation may be the start of a long-term or life-long partnership but the cohabitation period itself is rarely long-term.' Only about 5% of cohabitations last 10 years or more. Instead, 3 in 5 cohabitations will turn into marriage while the remainder are most likely to break down. Cohabiting relationships are four times more likely to break down than marriages, even when children are involved. Current analysis suggests that around 20% of today's young people will never marry: 'A succession of cohabiting unions and partnerships in which the two people live in separate residences will replace marriage for a large minority.'

Childbearing within cohabiting unions has become more common, with 22% of children being born into such unions in 1997, compared with 2% 20 years ago. However, far from being a reliable indicator of a stable relationship, becoming a mother actually reduces the odds of converting the cohabitation into marriage by 60%. And only 36% of children born to non-married couples will live their entire childhood with both natural parents (compared to 70% born within marriage).

It is estimated that approximately 40% of lone-parent families are created through the breakdown of cohabiting relationships and after parental separation, children are twice as likely to lose touch with their fathers if their parents had not married than if they had.

'The higher risk of experiencing their parents' partnership break-up that children born in cohabiting unions face is likely to be a cause for policy concern because of the difficulties faced when partnerships dissolve, particularly those that arise when the child is living with only one parent figure in the household.'

There is also evidence that pre-marital cohabitation can actually increase the chance of marriage breakdown later.

Proportion of the population by marital status[1] and gender[2]

Since the mid-1970s the proportion of the population that are married is not as large as it once was. While the proportion of men and women who are married has been declining, the proportions who are cohabiting have been increasing, and the proportion living outside a partnership has also increased.

Great Britain				Percentages
	1971	1981	1991	2000
Males				
Single	24	27	31	34
Married	71	66	60	53
Divorced	4	4	4	4
Widowed	1	3	6	8
All males[2]	100	100	100	100
Females				
Single	19	21	23	26
Married	65	61	56	52
Divorced	15	15	14	12
Widowed	1	4	7	9
All females[2]	100	100	100	100

1 Population estimated by marital status for 1971 are based on the 1971 Census and those for 1981 are based on the 1981 Census and have not been rebased using the 1991 Census
2 Adults aged 16 and over

Source: Office for National Statistics; General Register Office for Scotland

Divorce

In 1999 there were 145,000 divorces granted in England and Wales, continuing the downward trend generally seen since the peak in 1993. However the divorce rate rose marginally between 1998 and 1999 to 13 persons divorcing per 1,000 married population.

Of these divorcing couples, 55% had at least one child. The number of children under 16 experiencing divorce of their parents in 1999 was 148,000, one in four of whom were under 5 years old. 70% of all divorces in 1999 were granted to the wife.

Childbearing within cohabiting unions has become more common, with 22% of children being born into such unions in 1997, compared with 2% 20 years ago

---

The effect of divorce on children has been well documented. It is estimated that adverse outcomes are roughly twice as prevalent among children of divorced families compared with children from intact families. Furthermore, people who experience parental divorce are more likely to experience partnership and marriage dissolution themselves.

Some of the causes of increased marital breakdown may be linked to the following trends: 'The earlier a partnership is formed, the more likely it is to break down. Other demographic factors that have been implicated in marital breakdown include having a pre-marital birth, cohabiting prior to marriage and having a spouse who has previously been married.'

Please note: Due to space limitations the references for this article have been omitted. A full version of this article including references can be found at www.care.org.uk/resource/docs/res_familytrends.htm

© *CARE – Christian Action Research and Education*

Marriages up for the first time in eight years

By Celia Hall

The number of people getting married has gone up for the first time in eight years, partly because of the increasing numbers who marry for the second, third or more times.

Forty-two per cent of marriages involve at least one partner who has been married before, compared with 37 per cent a decade ago.

Marriages in which both the man and the woman have been married before went up to nearly one in five, 19 per cent, compared with 17 per cent in 1992.

The new data from National Statistics, *Population Trends 107*, Spring 2000, show that there were 263,515 marriages in England and Wales in 2000, a rise of nearly two per cent over 1999.

While religious ceremonies fell by four per cent in the same period, civil marriages, in a variety of settings, rose by five per cent.

A quarter of all civil marriages now take place in licensed venues other than register offices, an option permitted since the Marriage Act of 1994.

Hotels are the most popular venues and account for 57 per cent of all approved premises. Stately homes were the settings for eight per cent of such ceremonies.

Other popular venues, in preference to marriage rooms in austere municipal buildings, were halls, sports and leisure centres, museums and even educational establishments, the survey showed.

John Haskey, who conducted the marriages survey for the population trends review, said: 'One in six of all marriages in the year 2000 was in these approved premises. That is quite a sharp increase.'

> **While religious ceremonies fell by four per cent in the same period, civil marriages, in a variety of settings, rose by five per cent**

'As to whether the increase in the number of sites available to get married in has affected the overall number of marriages, it is impossible to say. These couples may have got married anyway.'

The figures also showed that people continue to marry later.

The average age is now 35 for a bridegroom and 32 for a bride.

For those marrying for the first time, a traditional church wedding is still popular.

Nearly half of marriages where both parties were marrying for the first time were religious ceremonies. This compares with 14 per cent where both parties had been married before and sought a religious wedding.

Mr Haskey, of the Office for National Statistics, said it was difficult to determine why there had been an

increase in marriages after so many years of falling numbers.

However, he stressed that the overall marriage rate, the ratio of the number of marriages to the overall population, continued to fall.

Although more people got married, there was also a growing population.

He also ruled out the possibility that more people had married in 2000 because of the millennium.

'We looked at the number of weddings around January but there was no sudden increase; the number of marriages rose throughout the year,' he said.

'I would be very dubious to talk about a millennium effect on the increase in marriages.'

The statistics also showed that the population is growing at a faster rate than previously predicted and that, based on current calculations, by 2025 there will be 65 million people living in the UK.

Chris Shaw, of the Government Actuary's Department, the body responsible for population projections, said two-thirds of the predicted increase would be through immigration.

He said the growth in population, which stood at 59.8 million in 2000, would be largely determined by more and more people moving to the UK rather than a natural change in births and deaths.

However, asylum seekers only accounted for a small proportion of that, estimated at around 20,000 per year, he added.

Mr Shaw also predicted that by 2040 the number of people dependent on the state – those of pensionable age or children aged under 16 – would be 700 for every 1,000 of the working population.

By 2007 the population of people of state pensionable age is expected to exceed the number of children aged under 16.

Marriage – raising questions, finding answers

Information from One Plus One Marriage and Partnership Research

One Plus One receives many questions relating to the following areas of research. The answers here cover some of the main points but are not exhaustive. If you would like more detailed research on a particular topic, search our library database or contact the information service at One Plus One.

Is marriage less popular today?

Rates for first marriages in Britain have been falling since the 1970s: in 1997 there were around 271,000 weddings in England and Wales, the lowest number this century. Yet surveys show that 83% of 10-17-year-olds still expect to marry (MORI, 1995).

Each year, more than 40% of weddings are remarriages for one or both partners, twice the level of 30 years ago

Younger people are less likely to marry, and to marry when older, than at any time previously. Many now live informally with a partner at an age when they would previously have been married. This has delayed, and to some extent replaced, marriage with cohabitation for people in their 20s. In England and Wales today, the average age at first marriage is 28 years for women and 30 years for men, compared with 24 years for women and 26 years for men in 1986.

However, it is important to note that there was an unprecedented rise in the popularity of marriage among young people after the war (in the early 1970s a third of brides were teenagers compared with 4% today). This was a result of economic affluence and of the social importance placed on marriage as conferring certain adult rights on young people: independence, regular sexual activity and the possibility of children.

Changing social attitudes have contributed to the acceptance of diverse relationship arrangements: living alone, with non-related significant others, cohabiting with a sexual partner, or in a non-committed sexual relationship, or marriage. There is less social and parental pressure to marry, although most people still think couples who want children should marry.

How is marriage different today?

Expectations of marriage have radically increased over the last 50 years, especially for women. There has been a shift in emphasis from the traditional segregated roles of 'home maker wife' and 'breadwinner husband' to an ideal based on equality and sharing; from marriage as an 'institution' based on instrumental, social and economic considerations to marriage as a 'companionate' ideal, in which self-fulfilment and personal growth are essential.

Women seem to have moved towards this 'relational' model faster than men, the women's movement being an important catalyst.

Are married or cohabiting relationships more at risk of breakdown?

Available evidence suggests that cohabitations are three to four times more likely to break down than marriages.

Cohabiting relationships can involve different degrees of commitment, whereas marriage presumes a certain common element of commitment. In a study of cohabiting mothers, when asked if they would choose the same partner again, three-quarters of those who were married replied positively, compared with only 56% of long-term cohabitees – indicating a greater degree of instability in cohabitations than in marriage.

Who has affairs?

The Sexual Attitudes and Lifestyles Survey in Britain estimates that 10% of married men and 5% of married women have had sex with someone other than their spouse in the previous five years. In 1996, 26% of divorces in England and Wales were granted on the grounds of adultery; 35% of those brought by men and 22% of those brought by women.

What are current attitudes to infidelity?

Most people still disapprove of extra-marital sex: 80-90% say they think it is 'mostly or always wrong' – almost the same as 20 years ago. In fact, 'faithfulness' still appears in the top three ingredients of a successful marriage, despite increasingly liberal attitudes towards other aspects of sexual behaviour. Around 62% of respondents to a 1995 European survey said they thought 'commitment to being faithful to your partner' was the most important definition of marriage.

Why do remarriages break down more than first marriages?

Most divorced people form new partnerships within a few years and many eventually remarry. In Britain, around half of all second marriages end in divorce, and nearly 60% of third marriages. The average age at remarriage is 38 for women and 41 for men. Remarriage rates are twice as high for men than women.

There are several reasons why remarriages are more divorce-prone:
- the existence of children from a previous relationship, and 'instant' parenthood for stepparents can be difficult; stepmothers particularly find part-time step-parenting challenging;

Cohabiting relationships can involve different degrees of commitment, whereas marriage presumes a certain common element of commitment

---

First marriages

Average age at first marriage in selected years, England and Wales.

Source: National Statistics, Crown copyright

- the breakdown of the first marriage may reflect a lack of skill in selecting a suitable partner;
- unresolved emotional or financial issues from the previous marriage may put the new marriage under pressure;
- some researchers argue that couples who have experienced divorce are more likely to see it as a way out of marital difficulties than first-time couples.

What do couples argue about?

Marital conflict is usually seen in negative terms, as signifying underlying problems in the relationship. However, some disagreement between partners is normal, representing an attempt to resolve the underlying issues of power and dependence that need to be resolved in every relationship. Frequency of conflict says relatively little about the quality of a relationship; it is the ability to manage conflicts and resolve issues of incompatibility that are important for marital satisfaction. Issues relating to communication, sex, jealousy, housework, finance and the like emerge most frequently in studies of marital conflict. However, the topics couples argue about are different according to their age, the duration of their relationship and what 'life stage' they have reached; for example, older people are more likely to be in longer relationships and at a particular life stage:

- middle-aged couples (40-50 years) are more likely to argue about children, money and communication in that order;
- for older couples (60-70 years), the major causes of disagreement are communication, recreation and money.

Factors influencing the course of marital conflict include compatibility between the partners, their personalities, their skills at resolving conflict, and the stressful circumstances they encounter.

Distressed couples argue in a different way to non-distressed couples, displaying more frequently and more intensely such behaviours as sarcasm, hostility, criticism and rejection.

Is marriage good for you?

A growing body of research has highlighted the health and health-related differences between married and unmarried people. For example:

- Married people have, on average, lower incidences of cancer, heart disease and strokes than divorced people.
- Supportive spouses aid recovery from illness, and married people have a lower rate of premature mortality than their divorced counterparts;
- Married people indulge less in 'risky' behaviours such as smoking, drinking and unsafe sex than divorced people. In 1998, the Health Education Authority in England launched a safer sex campaign aimed at divorced men, 40% of whom report two or more sexual partners over the previous year, compared to 2% of married men.

The effects of prolonged marital conflict on health are well documented. Kiecolt-Glaser et al (1998) report that negative conflict behaviours adversely affect both blood pressure and the immune system for up to 24 hours.

Marital problems increase the likelihood of depression, especially in women.

- The above information is an extract from One Plus One's web site: www.oneplusone.org.uk Alternatively see page 41 for their address details.

© One Plus One Marriage and Partnership Research

Young people's views

What do young people think about marriage and relationships?

In our changing social landscape, it is all too easy to assume a process of moral decline – but what do today's young people really think about marriage? How do they see their future lives as partners and as parents?

A publication launched today (Tuesday 23 October 2001) to mark Parents' Week suggests that rather than turning their backs on marriage, many young people want to wait until they are older to give their relationships a greater chance of success. As 13-year-old Kiera put it, 'You should just spend a while with whoever you're going to marry, make sure he's the right person and all, make sure he's going to be the right father for your children.'

More than just a piece of paper? Young people's views of marriage and relationships, published by the National Children's Bureau (NCB), illustrates the complexity of young people's ideas and experiences. Intended for a range of professionals, including teachers, youth workers and personal advisers, the resource aims to support young people in understanding their relationships and developing the skills to manage them.

The publication draws on findings from the Respect study, a major research project involving nearly 2,000 young people aged 11 to 16, funded by the Economic and Social Research Council (ESRC). Author Sue Sharpe also looks at previous research and examines the changing picture of marriage and the family over the years, particularly during the 20th century.

For many young people, marriage was seen as a choice rather than a must. The most popular option was the prospect of living with a partner, followed by the possibility of marriage – although a small minority of young women felt there was no point getting married at all. 'My mum's always saying, when you're older don't ever get married,' commented 14-year-old Lisa.

NATIONAL CHILDREN'S BUREAU

making a difference

Reasons cited by the young people for getting married included a sense of commitment and the apparent promise of security, including sexual security. 'I don't think the actual ceremony is particularly important, but I think marriage is a good thing. I think the stability it provides in the home is quite a good thing,' said Henry, one of a group of 15 and 16-year-old boys. The majority of young people also strongly supported the principle of marriage or relationships between people of different religions or cultures.

Many young people – especially young women – expressed a desire to fulfil other ambitions, such as completing their education or travelling the world, before committing to a long-term relationship. Others believed that it was important to have financial stability before embarking on marriage.

Questioned about divorce, almost all the young people felt that it was better for parents to separate rather than live together in conflict and hostility, although they considered that parents should make an effort to sort out their relationship first. Having to choose which parent to live with was identified as the most painful aspect of divorce or separation.

'Many young people growing up today have witnessed the making, breaking and remaking of adult relationships, and that has given them a different perspective on the lives they themselves are likely to lead,' commented Sue Sharpe. 'The challenge is to ensure that their experiences and needs lie at the heart of education about marriage and relationships. We need to move from a prescriptive approach to one that explores young people's ideas and encourages them to develop the skills they will need now and in the future.'

• The above information is an extract from the National Children's Bureau (NCB) web site which can be found at www.ncb.org.uk

© *The National Children's Bureau (NCB)*

The graph below shows the marriage expectations of never-married childless males and females aged under 35 in a cohabiting union in 1998. Nearly three-quarters of never-married childless people aged under 35 who were cohabiting expected to marry each other. Thus, for most people, cohabiting is part of the process of getting married and is not a substitute for marriage. About two-fifths of the cohabiting adults perceived advantages to just living together rather than marrying.

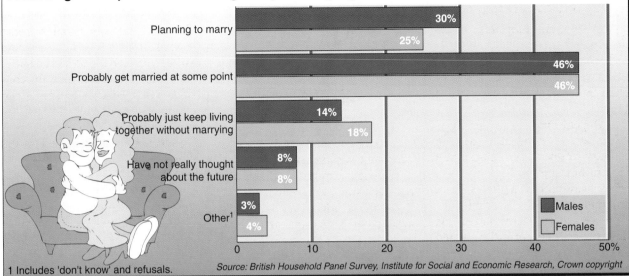

	Males	Females
Planning to marry	30%	25%
Probably get married at some point	46%	46%
Probably just keep living together without marrying	14%	18%
Have not really thought about the future	8%	8%
Other[1]	3%	4%

1 Includes 'don't know' and refusals.

Source: British Household Panel Survey, Institute for Social and Economic Research, Crown copyright

Live-in partners find love doesn't last

By Steve Doughty, Social Affairs Correspondent

One in four Britons in their early 30s has been through the break-up of a live-in relationship, it emerged yesterday.

Official figures show the generation which opted for cohabitation in place of marriage has suffered 'chronic family instability', leaving hundreds of thousands of children to be brought up by single parents.

The influential *General Household Survey* showed thirty-somethings who chose to marry were much more likely to stay together.

Only one in 12 of those in the age group who married has since divorced. More than 19,000 men and women were questioned by the Office for National Statistics.

It found that a third of live-in relationships lasts less than a year while a quarter failed to survive beyond two years.

Only one in ten lasts longer than five years.

On average, a cohabitation lasts 26 months with the toll for break-ups greatest among the 30 to 34 age group. Nearly a quarter had seen one relationship break up, one in 25 had been through two broken live-in relationships and one in 50 had had three or more.

Older people are more likely to have married. But even among those in their late 20s, one in five is a survivor of a broken live-in partnership.

Women with children are more likely to cohabit, the survey found. Nearly one in three – 31 per cent – of unmarried women with children was in a live-in relationship, compared with 23 per cent of unmarried women without children. The figures will be a blow to activists pressing for a law to give live-in couples the same property rights as married ones.

Liberal Democrat Peer Lord Lester, QC, introduced a Private Member's Bill last week to give legal status to 'civil partnerships' – a move widely regarded as a test for future legislation.

Yesterday's figures show, however, that, far from being a modern and rational alternative to marriage, most cohabitation is unstable and short-lived. Sociologist Patricia Morgan, author of the *Marriage Lite* study of cohabitation, said yesterday: 'Cohabitation is a transitory and fragile state and produces single parent families.

'People don't enter it because they want commitment but because they want to be able to get out easily and early.' She added: 'A cohabitation law would mean a huge payday for lawyers.

'They would land an enormous amount of work – much of it paid for by the taxpayer through legal aid.'

© *The Daily Mail*
January, 2002

9

Get hitched for health and happiness

Be warned: marriage could seriously improve your health. At least, that's what the researchers say. In fact, research consistently shows that overall, both men and women fare better when they are married. They are generally healthier, happier and more fulfilled.

Forsaking all others

Marriage exerts a strong influence on faithfulness within a relationship. A much lower proportion of married couples report sexual relationships outside their marriage than those who cohabit.

For raising children

Marriage provides the most stable and enduring environment in which to raise children. It also encourages people to take on greater responsibility for their offspring. Marriage is the child's best defence against being in a household lower on the income scale.

Even where there are children, half of cohabiting couples part within 10 years, compared to just 1 in 8 married parents. Only 45% of children of cohabiting couples stay in touch with both parents after a break-up, compared with 69% of those who were married

For richer, for poorer

Marriage recognises that the wider society is involved and has a stake in the family unit. All families rely on healthcare, financial support for those in need and education for children. In turn, society depends on the stability, cohesiveness and financial security of the family.

The break-up of relationships causes immense personal distress and damage that reverberates out into the social sphere and into the public purse. The stability of the family is of crucial importance to the well-being of society.

Marriage also provides the most committed relationship within which to share the support and care for a wider group of people – such as the elderly, disabled or other members of the extended family. That level of commitment is less likely to be found in the looser arrangement of cohabitation.

In sickness and in health

Numerous studies have shown that married people live longer and are emotionally and physically healthier than the unmarried. For example, research has found that cohabitors are more likely to exhibit depression and drunkenness than married persons. Married people also spend less time in bed due to acute illness and are 8-17% more likely to survive cancer than unmarried people (RH Coombs/*Family Relations* 1991).

Research has consistently found that physical aggression is more common among cohabiting couples than married couples. Some research has shown it to be at least twice as common – 35% of cohabiting couples have experienced physical aggression compared to 15% of married couples (J Stets/*Journal of Marriage and the Family*).

There are many studies indicating that married people are, on average, happier than the unmarried, for example, one study found that 61% of married people were satisfied with life compared to 49% of cohabiting people (*Bulletin Plus*, One Plus One 1997).

Till death us do part

Despite claims to the contrary, cohabitation is, on the whole, a poor substitute and an ineffective trial for marriage. Studies show that cohabiting couples are almost six times as likely to split up as those who are

---

There are many studies indicating that married people are, on average, happier than the unmarried

---

married (*British Household Panel Survey* as reported in *The Guardian*, 1 December 1995) and pre-marital cohabitation significantly increases the risk of marriage breakdown, such marriages are twice as likely to end than marriages without premarital cohabitation (*Social Trends 24*; *Population Trends* 68, 1992).

In cohabitation the door is always ajar. There is no life-long commitment and the option of breaking up is consciously preserved. There will inevitably be insecurity within such a relationship.

Marriage – the relevant relationship

For most people nowadays, marriage means weddings, enormous expense and considerable pressure. Yet the Bible doesn't prescribe the nature of the celebration. What it does do, however, is lay down the theological and legal essentials of marriage.

The marriage relationship provides the God-given ideal setting for the natural desire of men and women to find a companion. It is the place where sexual expression and family life are best protected by the security and stability that are provided by mutual commitment.

There are sociologists who believe marriage is just a particular phase in social evolution that will eventually become extinct – and is beginning to be outdated already. All experiments to try and extinguish the marriage bond will fail because the need and desire for the special pair bonding of marriage will always be there, as God intended.

If the permanent commitment of marriage is undetermined and if people ignore the clear guidelines laid down by God then our whole society will suffer.

• The above information is an extract from *Virtual Marriage*, produced by CARE. See page 41 for their address details. ©CARE – *Christian Action Research and Education*

The truth about marriage

Younger men yearn for affection. Yes, the seven-year itch really does exist and a quarter of married people wouldn't do it again

Have you ever hidden a price tag from your spouse? Suppressed a secret desire or just wished you weren't married any more? With 40% of British marriages now heading for divorce, MORI conducted an exclusive *Reader's Digest* Poll of married people looking at their attitudes towards marriage, their experiences and how honest and open they are with each other.

The survey was conducted by MORI who interviewed 971 married adults aged 16 years and over throughout Great Britain. The findings are revealed in the January issue of *Reader's Digest*.

Russell Twisk, Editor-in-Chief of *Reader's Digest* says: 'What a confusing picture. Men wanting to talk more – we'd always thought it was women. Men longing for affection and wishing they could talk about sex. A surprising number of women kept in ignorance about how much their partners earn. Proof that the seven-year itch really does exist.

'Yet middle-aged couples are five times more likely to fantasise about having a dog than dream of an extra-marital affair. The state of marriage in Britain 2002 is puzzling and contradictory – for over a quarter of British married couples say that given their experience of it they would NOT get married again!'

Among the survey's findings are:

What can't couples talk about?
Some of the poll's greatest surprises arise from conversations married people wish they could have but don't – especially younger men.

Lighten up
- 44% of men under 45 wish they could talk to their partner about having more fun.

More togetherness
- 40% of men under 45 wish they could talk to their partner about spending more time together.

More sex
- 29% of men under 45 wish they could talk about their sex lives, compared with 17% of women.

More cuddles
- 22% of men under 45 wish they could ask their partner to be more affectionate.

Seven-year itch – fact not fiction
- 30% of people married between six and nine years confess that they've wished they could wake up one morning and not be married any more.

- 30% of men married for nine years or less wish they could talk about their sex lives – compared with 12% of women.

What are our most-kept secrets?
- Money is a major taboo area – 20% (one in five) of those who have been married for 20-29 years have no idea how much their spouse has saved or invested or even how much their partner earns.
- 44% of women and 39% of men confess they have kept something secret from their partners.

Attitudes towards marriage
- Over a quarter (27%) of married people say that given their experience, they would not get married again.

Do couples share their dreams?
- Nearly one in five (18 per cent) admit they have at some point had dreams or aspirations they do not talk about with their spouse.

• MORI conducted 971 face-to-face interviews with married people aged 16+, in 192 sampling points in Great Britain, between 4 and 9 October 2001. MORI's web site can be found at www.mori.com

© MORI (Market & Opinion Research International Limited)

Children pay the price when their parents don't marry

By Jill Kirby

The Government's ministerial group on the family, launched in 1998 to show its commitment to 'joined-up thinking' on family issues, has been closed down. David Blunkett, chairman of the sub-committee that replaces it, has reportedly agreed 'not to reopen the debate on the subject of marriage and family structure'. Family structure has become a no-go zone for British politicians.

Yet there is now a massive weight of evidence on the matter that needs to be discussed. This evidence shows that children brought up outside two-parent families are at a persistent disadvantage, and that the length of time a couple stays together is firmly linked to marriage.

The Government presumably wishes to avoid talking about these issues because such a discussion would require an explicit declaration on the importance of marriage, a declaration that would split the Cabinet.

For the Tories, the subject is also fraught. While in government, they reduced fiscal support for the married family to a bare minimum, making it easy for Gordon Brown later to abandon what little remained of the married couple's allowance.

In opposition, there have been more encouraging signs, although reticence persists. Oliver Letwin, the shadow home secretary, has alluded to the role of family in building the neighbourly society, but he has yet to be drawn on the role of government in supporting it.

The problem will not go away. The number of children born outside marriage continues to rise, and now stands at 40 per cent of all births in this country. Those who claim that family life is merely changing, not declining, or that cohabitation is 'the new marriage', are ignoring the facts.

Cohabitation is a transient condition. Within five years of the birth of a child, 52 per cent of cohabitees have split up, compared with just eight per cent of married couples. It is estimated that a quarter of all children in Britain are living in lone-parent families, twice as many as in France or Germany.

It is therefore increasingly urgent that the prospects of those children be discussed. There is no lack of British data, and the picture is bleak from babyhood onwards.

The children of lone parents are twice as likely to have mental health problems than the children of married couples

Infant mortality is substantially higher for children of lone or cohabiting parents than for those of married parents, babies born outside marriage are more likely to have low birth weights, to suffer childhood accidents, and to be at much higher risk of child abuse.

The children of lone parents are twice as likely to have mental health problems than the children of married couples.

A series of British long-term studies has shown a steady con-nection between broken homes and delinquency, as well as a greater propensity to youth crime among children born to teenage mothers and those whose parents have split up.

According to a report in 1998 by the Joseph Rowntree Foundation, children of separated families are twice as likely to have behavioural problems, perform less well in school, become sexually active at a younger age, suffer depression and turn to drugs, smoking and heavy drinking.

Dispelling a common myth, the report also concluded that the death of a parent is less damaging to a child's long-term welfare than parental divorce or separation.

The Children's Society last year disclosed that children living in step-families are three times more likely to run away from home than children living with both their natural parents; children of lone parents are twice as likely to do so. Many of these children end up on the streets.

Because a growing proportion of children are missing out on the experience of growing up with two committed parents, they lack a model on which to build their own lives.

So girls from broken families are almost twice as likely as their contemporaries to become teenage lone mothers, and children who experience parental separation are much more likely to have their own adult relationships break up.

The ever-increasing emotional and behavioural cost to the children

of broken families should be reason enough to press for a new approach to family policy; there are also huge financial implications.

As the married family declines, so an increasing welfare burden must be shouldered by such families. The latest figures show that 73 per cent of lone parents are in receipt of income support, compared with 11 per cent of couples with children.

While the numbers of lone parents continue to rise, the Government's desire to end child poverty must remain an impossible dream, for where the state intervenes by financing alternatives to the married family, so the number of broken families rises and the demands on the state increase.

Policy in other areas is based on the assumption that taxes affect behaviour. High fuel taxes are meant to discourage us from using our cars; cigarettes and alcohol are taxed to stop us smoking and drinking.

Yet, in contrast to most other European economies, governments here have refused to adopt this approach to family taxation or to welfare benefits. We have instead a system that is an incentive for child neglect.

A programme of reform is urgently needed to restore family stability. We could start by educating children about the value of marriage and enduring fatherhood.

We need to remove from the welfare structure the existing disincentives to marriage and committed parenting. In terms of tax, we must restore recognition of marriage, preferably following the French or German example of offering joint taxation, combined with a system of family allowances.

But until our politicians are prepared to discuss the consequences of family collapse, the prospect of any of these changes is remote indeed.

In America, the overwhelming weight of evidence on the link between broken homes, fatherlessness and crime has brought about a change in attitude, inspiring cross-party support for pro-marriage initiatives. Recent statistics there show that these initiatives are beginning to stem family decline.

In Britain, by contrast, we seem to have a cross-party consensus for silence on the 'M word'.

• Jill Kirby chairs a family policy group at the Centre for Policy Studies and is the author of *Broken Hearts – Family Decline and the Consequences for Society*

Marriages make a millennium comeback

By Nicole Martin

The millennium year saw the number of couples getting married rise for the first time since 1992, according to the latest Government figures.

There were 267,961 marriages in England and Wales in 2000, compared with 263,515 in 1999, the Office for National Statistics said yesterday.

The rise of almost two per cent reverses a trend that had seen the number of marriages steadily falling from a peak of 311,564 in 1992. Experts yesterday attributed the increase to the millennium, which many couples viewed as a memorable time to marry.

They said it was also possible that more people were taking advantage of changes in legislation allowing couples to marry in 'approved premises' such as hotels, stately homes and football clubs rather than register offices.

They said that the Marriage Act 1994, which was introduced to extend the number and variety of civil wedding locations, gave non-religious couples the opportunity to make their wedding unique.

The figures showed that since the change in legislation, the proportion of religious marriage ceremonies, which had been steady at around half for decades, has fallen to 36 per cent. In 2000 there were 97,161 religious ceremonies compared with 100,836 in 1999.

Meanwhile, the number of civil ceremonies rose from 162,679 in 1999 to 170,800 in 2000 – 64 per cent of all marriages, compared with 52 per cent in 1994.

Of those, more than a quarter were conducted in approved places, reflecting the growing trend to marry in places other than churches or register offices. In 1996 fewer than one in 10 civil marriages were in approved premises.

Among the approved venues are Sir Christopher Wren's house in Windsor, Caerphilly Castle, Knebworth Park in Hertfordshire, Aston Villa football club and Cheltenham racecourse.

Denise Knowles, a counsellor for the marriage guidance charity Relate, said: 'Many people wanted to marry in the millennium, in the same way that many people wanted a millennium baby. It's possible that couples saw it as a time for a big change and for starting again.'

A spokesman for the Church of England said: 'I hope that people are getting married with serious intentions and a commitment to making it a life-long union.'

The Government figures also showed that people were choosing to marry later, with the average age for bridegrooms rising from 34.4 years in 1999 to 34.8 years in 2000. For brides, the corresponding rise was from 31.8 to 32.1

Marriage and living together

Information from youthinformation.com by the National Youth Agency

You and your partner may decide to live together or get married. Living together all the time is very different from going out together. It can cause problems if you expect different things – for instance sharing the cooking or housework. It's a good idea to talk about these things beforehand and review them from time to time to see if you both still agree.

If you want to get married you can either have a religious or civil (non-religious) ceremony.

Religious wedding ceremonies

A religious ceremony can take place at a church or chapel of the Church of England or any other place of worship which has been registered by the Registrar General for marriages. If you want to marry in a church of the Church of England then you need to go and see the vicar who will tell you whether or not you can be married in the church. If you can then the vicar will usually make arrangements to register the marriage.

For other religious ceremonies you will need to see the person responsible for marriages at the church or temple where you plan to get married. This should normally be in the area where you live. You will also have to give notification of your marriage to the registrar in the district where you live.

If you want to have a religious ceremony where there is no authorised person present then you will have to have a civil ceremony on a separate occasion.

Civil wedding ceremony

A civil ceremony can take place at a register office or other approved place for marriage (such as a hotel). You will need to contact the superintendent registrar in the district where you wish to get married and later give formal notice that you plan to get married. If you have any questions about marriage, particu-larly about the timing, contact the local register office for marriages.

A useful leaflet, *Getting Married: a guide to weddings in England and Wales*, published by the General Register Office/Office of Population Censuses and Surveys (May 1995), explains the details.

Under the law, being married and living together are not seen as the same thing. Marriage involves a signed contract and understanding between two people which takes place at the marriage ceremony. This agreement gives both partners certain rights in the marriage.

Two people living together who are not married do not usually have a written agreement between them and the law is not so precise in the rights of one or other partner in the event of dispute or break-up of the relationship.

For example, being married means that the couple have, by law, to support each other. This can even extend outside marriage, if the couple divorce. These financial responsibilities do not usually apply to unmarried couples living together.

Both married and unmarried parents do have a responsibility to support their children, however, including a continuing responsibility if the marriage breaks down. Both unmarried and married caring parents have equal rights to apply to the Child Support Agency.

Another important difference is that married couples have joint responsibility for any children as long as they were married to each other at the time of the child's birth. Unmarried fathers do not have parental responsibility, unless both parents have signed a parental responsibility agreement or there is an order of court.

A spouse (i.e. partner in marriage) who is not the legal owner or tenant of the home where the married couple are living, none-theless has a legal right to live in it under the 1983 Matrimonial Act.

Unmarried couples do not have any rights to occupy the home under the 1983 Act. However, both married and unmarried couples should get legal advice about their rights to a property before they rent or purchase it.

You can get married if you and your partner are over 16 (and not already married!). If you are under 18 and want to marry then you will need the written agreement of your parents. Marriages where both or one of the partners is under 16, or between two people of the same sex (even if one has had a sex change) are illegal.

Being married to more than one person at the same time (known as bigamy) is usually illegal. This is not the case if you married abroad under the laws of a country which permit a man to have more than one wife.

Engagement is no longer a contract under law. Until 1970 it was, and anyone breaking an engagement was liable to be sued for damages. Now it has no impact in a court of law – even the engagement ring is seen as a gift!

• The above information is from www.youthinformation.com which is run by the National Youth Agency See page 41 for their address details.

© 2002 National Youth Agency

Death of marriage

It will be all but extinct in 30 years, says Relate

By Sarah Harris,
Education Reporter

Marriage is doomed and will be virtually extinct within 30 years, according to the country's leading relationship experts.

They say the vast majority of couples will reject it in favour of a series of long-term relationships.

Ironically, the prediction comes from Relate, which used to be called the Marriage Guidance Council.

Duncan White, who is in charge of Relate's 2,000 counsellors, believes that only one in five long-term couples will be married by 2030, and at least eight in ten births will be outside marriage.

If partners do eventually tie the knot it will be only to make a social statement or to gain a rewarding tax break.

Speaking before the British Association for Counselling and Psychotherapy conference in Nottingham yesterday, he said that his staff were seeing vast changes in the way people view marriage.

'It will be seen as an esoteric choice rather than the norm,' he said.

Instead he forecast an increase in 'constellation' relationships where couples have a series of long-term relationships with children from each.

Annual wedding rates are now at their lowest since records began 160 years ago, while 40 per cent of marriages are doomed to failure, the conference heard.

Divorce is running at 160,000 a year, also thought to represent an all-time high.

And while 20 years ago one in eight babies was born outside wedlock, this had risen steadily to four in ten by 2000.

Relate's Julia Cole, a psychosexual therapist, added that increasing involvement in affairs would also damage the idea of marriage.

'Affairs are not necessarily the death-knell for the couple, but they are a warning that urgent attention is required if the relationship is to survive,' she told the conference.

Christopher Clulow, director of the Tavistock Marital Studies Institute, agreed that more and more couples now prefer to live together.

They also favour marrying at register offices, hotels and stately homes rather than having a traditional church ceremony, he said.

Breaking up 'is child abuse'

Family breakdown is akin to child abuse, a leading researcher has claimed.

Dr Clifford Hill said virtually every persistent juvenile offender comes from a broken home while millions of youngsters have serious problems.

Dr Hill, of the Family Matters Institute, told a London conference: 'The suffering of children from broken homes needs to be recognised as child abuse on a massive scale.

'Yet we get fiercely defensive at any suggestion that single parents don't do as good a job as married couples'.

Mr Clulow said: 'More than three in five women marrying for the first time already live with their husband-to-be.

'Around half of all conceptions take place outside marriage, and in excess of one in three births are to unmarried women.

'There can be no clearer indications of the trend to deregulate marriage than falling marriage rates and the increasing practice of cohabitation.'

Mr Clulow added: 'The regulation of marriage by church and state is receding. Two-thirds of weddings will be civil rather than religious events.

'A quarter of these will take place in "approved premises" other than register offices – hotels, stately homes and so on.

'This deregulation is also evident in the lessening of social sanctions on divorce. Around two in five marriages are predicted to end in divorce, which will affect on in three of all children by their 16th birthday.'

• The Marriage Guidance Council was founded in 1938 by clergyman Dr Herbert Gray to help husbands and wives sort out their problems.

© The Daily Mail
April, 2002

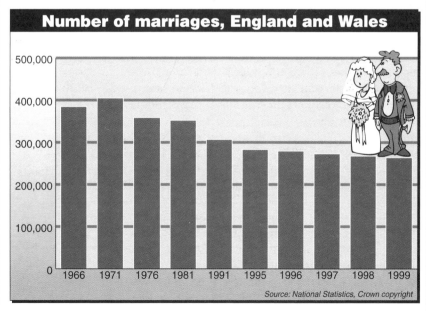

Number of marriages, England and Wales

Source: National Statistics, Crown copyright

Marriage is for love, not life

By Jeanette Winterson

Spring is here, and every marquee in the Cotswolds has been hired out for a wedding. Marriage is back in fashion. There is always a spring rush, but business is booming. My gym is plastered with notices urging me to visit the Juliet and Desdemona bridal collection. I know I live near Stratford-upon-Avon, and the bard can sell anything in Britain, from tea towels to Quill Fries (they come in a bag with a picture of Anne Hathaway cooking them in her cottage), but suppose the bride made the mistake of reading the plays? Maybe you get a free phial of poison with every wedding dress. Perhaps today's Desdemona will strangle Othello before he has a chance to be eaten up with jealousy.

Maybe I'm misreading the whole thing and Juliet and Desdemona are marrying each other in California, and Romeo and Othello are opening a bar. But if Britain really is becoming more matrimonial, we have broken off our love affair with everything American, where the annual number of weddings per 1,000 eligible women has fallen by a third since the 1970s.

During the 1990s, the number of unmarried-partner households in America increased by over 70%. Is this just the land of the free getting freer? Might it be that women don't want to marry in the way they once did – perhaps because economic independence means they don't need to marry?

It has been said that marriage survives because it is a very efficient way for people to organise their common lives together – children, money, property, all get taken care of without too much thought. Add in emotional security and social approval, and marriage looks good – at least on paper.

In the US, the problems for marriage seem to be less about feminism or pay parity, and more about the paper benefits of marriage becoming less important. The stigma attached to unmarried relationships is gone, and because conservative groups don't want gay people to marry, a whole raft of legal concessions has been put in place to keep gay partnerships afloat – the unintended effect being that unmarried heterosexuals benefit too.

> **Marriage isn't for life any more – life is too long. Marriage is for love. Love gladly accepts responsibility. Love wants commitment**

If you can get everything that marriage offers without marrying – why marry? The paradox is that countries that have genuinely equal partnership laws, such as Denmark and Sweden, have not experienced a sharp decline in marriage. America's desperate attempt not to rock the boat is in peril of sinking the ship. Marriage has become unsexy, and dangerously undemocratic. If society as a whole benefits from marriage, as its supporters claim, marriage has to be an option for every member of society, regardless of sexual orientation.

Rightwingers hate this kind of talk, but then rightwingers have been against mixed marriages, marriages to non-virgins, cross-class marriages, non-religious ceremonies, no-fault divorce and, of course, second marriages. Rightwingers have been proved wrong every time – society has not collapsed, society continues to evolve. Even *Country Life*, not known as the vanguard magazine for alternative lifestyles, recently ran an editorial rejoicing in Britain's rising marriage rate, then admitted these statistics related to second marriages.

Marriage isn't for life any more – life is too long. Marriage is for love. Love gladly accepts responsibility. Love wants commitment. Marriage should be celebrated as the optimistic and glorious thing that it is. We can't call it a failure if it doesn't last for ever.

The only failure is cynicism. The US government has just set aside $300m to try and persuade young men to marry their girlfriends instead of living with them. Meanwhile, the Bush administration is slashing or freezing welfare benefits to single mothers. This depressing right-wing route to a 1950s-style society, diluted with a bit of added tolerance, assumes that there really was something called 'the good ol' days' and that if we could only find our way back to Eden, we could all live happily ever after and sin no more.

Yet the fact that many young people do not choose marriage, is surely because their parents' marriages were so bloody awful. Why would you willingly put yourself in a situation shaped by misery?

Making marriage attractive again will cost more than tax breaks and PR. Instead of expecting us to fit ourselves into a frankly dodgy little number – and that's just the Desdemona wedding dress – let's make marriage the true centre of society and open it to everyone. Until then, it's never going to work.

Loosening the knot

Mark Oliver looks at what the government's shake-up of civil weddings, announced today, means for the future of marriage

What is expected to change?

The changes proposed in a government white paper hinge on making the person conducting the ceremony licensed, rather than the wedding venue itself.

Register office officials will be empowered as 'celebrants', who will be responsible for ensuring the chosen venue is safe and appropriate.

What will this mean?

It will clear the way for weddings to be held in places such as a private home, garden, mountain top or beach. At present ceremonies can only be held in a church, register office or specially licensed venue. The proposals – which apply to England, Wales and Northern Ireland – will be unveiled by the office for national statistics this afternoon.

Does this mean I will be able to get married hanging from a bungee cord?

No. It is thought that the more eccentric options, such as tying the knot while skydiving or bungee jumping from a military helicopter while decked out in Elvis costumes, will still not be approved. So you can forget your nuclear submarine wedding fantasy.

By Mark Oliver

What is the law now?

Couples were allowed to marry outside register offices for the first time following the previous biggest shake-up in civil ceremonies, the Marriage Act 1994. Currently, venues must apply to the local authority for a licence, which is only granted if the premises are deemed 'seemly and dignified'.

In practice, people considering a civil ceremony had the choice of taking their vows in venues including stately homes, castles or hotels. The 1994 act also removed the rule that couples must marry in the district in which one of them was resident.

How have people been using the current rules?

Many celebrity couples have taken advantage of the 1994 reforms and chosen to get married in private venues. Westlife star Bryan McFadden and former Atomic Kitten Kerry Katona recently wed in a lavish ceremony at Slane Castle in Ireland.

However, you do not need to be famous to have your special day in an unusual or eyebrow-arching venue. Simon Stapleton and Dawn Bottom-

ley, both from Burgess Hill, West Sussex, last year became the first couple to be married on the London Eye.

Two years ago, Geoff Williams and Catherine Ferris married 60m (200ft) underground in the Poldark tin mine near Helston in Cornwall. And Avril Thomson and her bridegroom David Blades, from Androssan in Ayrshire, had their big day in the Blue Lagoon in the Bahamas in 1998. A male dolphin was the best man and two female dolphins were the bridesmaids. The minister wore flippers.

Perhaps less exotically, Deborah Lane and Damien Clapp became the first British couple to marry in a shopping mall when they tied the knot at the Belfry centre in Redhill, Surrey, in 1999. Around 1,000 shoppers stopped perusing the aisles to watch the happy couple.

How has the Church responded to today's news of a further reduction of restrictions on marriage venues? Surely it's bad news for churches?

The Church of England said it was not worried that the new proposals would trivialise wedding ceremonies. 'We would love everyone to get married in church but, wherever they hold the ceremony, it's the marriage bit that matters,' a spokesman said.

He added that the Church of England has 16,000 of the best wedding venues in the country. He said: 'Between 60,000 and 70,000 couples choose them every year and we are not worried that these proposals will have an effect on church weddings.'

But does any of this matter? We keep hearing about the decline of marriage. What are the figures?

The government is keen to support marriage and a cynic might say that relaxing the rules on venues is just a gimmick to this end. Whereas 15 years ago there were 350,000 marriages a year now it is closer to only 250,000 with 145,000 divorces each year.

Only a quarter of marriages take place in a church or place of worship. However, marriage remains popular as an institution although nearly 40% of marriages are second marriages for either or both of the couple. The average length of a marriage that ends in divorce is currently 10 years.

The rules are different for Scotland. What is happening there?

In Scotland the executive has already unveiled proposals to relax the rules on where civil weddings can take place. The marriage (Scotland) bill was published last November and has been debated at stage one in the Scottish parliament.

Couples choosing a civil ceremony north of the border are currently restricted to Scotland's 247 register offices, however those opting for a religious ceremony have long been free to select any location providing their chosen celebrant agrees to it. Under the proposed legislation civil weddings could take place in castles, on boats and in gardens.

Is there any legislation afoot to change laws for unmarried couples?

The government is reportedly keen to give fresh attention to reforming the law on unmarried couples and is currently reviewing the whole issue. However, the pace of reform would appear to be cautious. Ministers last week rejected calls to back a private member's bill launched by Lord Lester of Herne Hill, a Liberal

Democrat peer, on giving civil partnerships equal rights.

So how far is the government prepared to go?

Well, there is talk of removing questions about whether applicants for state benefits are married and the introduction of other legal rights.

The cabinet office spokesman said last week that ministers were taking a 'very cross-cutting look at current financial and administrative issues' concerning whether gay and unmarried couples should be entitled to benefits.

Under the existing law, unmarried people who lose their partners do not benefit from inheritance tax allowances available to married couples. They also do not have a right to be involved in decisions involving the withdrawal of life support from terminally-ill partners.

Marriage remains popular as an institution although nearly 40% of marriages are second marriages for either or both of the couple

---

What is the latest on gay marriages?

Many believe the advent of homosexual marriages is inevitable as Britain broadly evolves into a more tolerant society. In the short term, gay couples are likely to gain from any of the benefits that unmarried couples receive.

Last year, the first gay couple were given the right to register their union by the mayor of London, Ken Livingstone. Ian Burford, a retired actor, and Alexander Cannell, a nursing manager, who had been together for 38 years, marked their commitment by registering themselves with the Greater London Authority as a couple.

The ceremony costs £85 and is open to both homosexual and heterosexual couples, as long as one partner lives in London. The document has no legal standing, although Mr Livingstone said he hoped that would change and the couple said it was a step in the direction of gay marriages. Stonewall, a gay rights pressure group, has long been pressing for equal recognition of homosexual couples over tax and pensions. The group would give unmarried partners equal tax and benefit rights, including the right to widows' pensions.

I do, I do, I do, I do . . .

Suddenly it's chic to marry. But how many of today's brides and grooms are old hands at the altar?

By Ben Summerskill

'Dearly beloved, we have come together in the presence of God to witness and bless the joining together of this man and this woman in Holy Matrimony.' The news that marriage is on the rise, after years of decline, has brought a smile to many who rejoice in the opening words of the marriage ceremony.

And what better time than Easter week to mark a revival of one of organised religion's biggest crowd-pullers?

After years in which 'family values' campaigners have bemoaned the decline of wedlock, the number of marriages in England and Wales rose in 2000 from 263,000 to almost 268,000. Statisticians say the trend will continue all this decade. 'Marriage in fashion again', said a typically approving headline last week.

That's the good news for the traditionalists. The less good news is that the figures are being boosted as much by people like Liza Minnelli and Joan Collins – 'serial mono-gamists' as sociologists put it – as by young couples embarking on a lifetime of exclusive commitment.

The number of weddings where one partner has been married before has risen above 40 per cent for the first time. And at one in five weddings, both bride and groom have good reason to be word-perfect – they will both have attended their own weddings in the past.

Tessa Field, 50, from Leeds, who first married in 1970, typifies our changing attitudes to marriage: 'I was pregnant and 19 and my boyfriend was 21,' she said. 'We were wed in church. I got married more for everyone else than for me, although you didn't say so in those days. We were so excited we just went along with it.

'My second wedding was after we'd been living together for a few years. We already had children by then. We went ahead even though I didn't think it was going to last.'

It didn't. After separating from her second husband two years ago, Field now lives with the best man from her first wedding. 'We were thinking of marrying, too, but I've put it off for the moment. I'll do it if it feels right. It's just not essential.'

> *At one in five weddings, both bride and groom have good reason to be word-perfect – they will both have attended their own weddings in the past.*

Once, the most significant glue to many marriages was social disapproval of single parenthood, divorce and living 'out of wedlock'. Those imperatives have declined dramatically in the last 30 years. A recent *British Social Attitudes* survey found that only a quarter of Britons thought married couples made better parents than unmarried ones.

One of the most remarkable shifts demonstrated by last week's figures from the Office for National Statistics is that civil marriages – with no religious component – now account for three in five weddings, up from just under half in 1991. That trend has been encouraged by the licensing since 1994 of thousands of 'approved premises' from golf clubs to stately homes so that civil ceremonies no longer have to take place in churches or – often staid and unwelcoming – register offices.

Christians were certainly not the first to solemnise marriage. Thousands of years earlier, pagan rituals regularised partnership between adults, particularly those rearing children. Christianity elevated the relationship, but along with religious endorsement came some of the ideological baggage so many younger people now disdain.

In his letter to the Ephesians, part of the purportedly progressive New Testament, St Paul wrote: 'A husband is the head of his wife, as Christ is the head and saviour of the Church. Wives should always put their husbands first.' It was only just over a decade ago that women marrying in the Church of England were first permitted not to pledge to 'obey' their new husbands.

'We wanted to get married as a sign of commitment to each other. Our motivation wasn't religious at all,' said Janet Kay, a 42-year-old broker from Sussex who has one daughter with her husband, Josh. 'It's just the next thing you do after a long-term relationship. We didn't do it because we'd had a child.'

Josh has one son from a previous relationship. Janet had been married twice for less than five years. The couple married in a register office last summer. 'Of course it's serious and of course we want it to last,' he said. 'We both believe we'll be together for the rest of our lives and I really hope that happens. But I'd be deeply dishonest to claim that it definitely will.

'It's not just a case of having been there before with relationships. There's far too much flam talked about marriage. I'm sure that a part of that is generational. Fifty years ago, even if people weren't happily married they pretended to be. We're able to be more realistic and practical. We're also able to recognise that there are benefits to marriage, but disbenefits too.'

Philip Hodson, of the British Association for Counselling and Psychotherapy, said: 'We live in troubled times. When you think of population migrations and global warming and threats to the food supply, it concentrates the mind. People have a wish to nurture each other through that.

'Detached from strictures of religion, they are being more realistic. People are still looking for allies and good friends in life. It's acceptable to say nowadays that no one is ready for marriage in their early twenties. People recognise that you aren't ready for a final commitment until you've had your heart broken and flexed your muscles.'

The average age of marriage is now 35 for men and 32 for women, compared with 28 and 26 a decade ago. A quarter of children are now born to cohabiting couples, often before they marry. 'Don't forget,' says Hodson, 'that 300 years ago, life expectancy was 32 years. Now 70 is the new 50. People are looking for quality of life, and sex, with or without Viagra, until their graves. People are adapting their marital lives to that ambition.'

The confirmation that religious weddings are in decline will reopen the festering sore within the Church of England over its accessibility to those who do wish to get married. Some priests still refuse to wed couples not living in their own parish, even if they were brought up there. Others have started offering wedding services to divorcees, an issue as painfully divisive to clerics as discrimination against gays.

Those priests who welcome divorcees may simply be recognising that, if institutions prove to be sclerotic, people adopt their own pick-and-mix approach to them. A keenness on spiritual values may be alive and healthy in Britain, but is often informed by a robust consumerism.

'We wanted to marry in a spiritual context,' said Janet Kay. 'We recognise that our lives are part of something greater. However, as the church in which we would have married was not prepared to recognise us as equal to other married couples, and as they had made an issue of us

already having a child, we just went somewhere else.'

'I'm cynical when I see recently married people like Liza Minnelli talking about how wonderful marriage is,' said Tessa Field. 'Nowadays you almost take it for granted that it's going to end in divorce. Almost one in two marriages now fails, so you're realistic about it. If it does work, of course that's great.'

• This article first appeared in *The Observer*, 31 March 2002.

Second-timers are bringing marriage back into fashion

By Steve Doughty

The number of couples getting married has gone up for the first time in eight years. Nearly 268,000 weddings were held in the year 2000, up from 263,000 in a rise of nearly two per cent on the year before.

The sudden upturn ends a long period of decline – during which governments stripped away all the tax privileges of marriage and some of its legal status – and may herald a revival for marriage, officials said.

But the biggest boom in wedding numbers came among older people who were going into marriage for a second time, according to yesterday's figures.

Some 58 per cent of weddings were first-time for both bride and groom, compared with 63 per cent in 1991. The figures mean that more divorcees or widows are now entering second marriages, while the number of couples embarking on the first marriage appears to have stabilised after years of decline.

John Haskey of the Office for National Statistics, which published the figures, said they could show the beginning of a reversal of the decline of marriage.

'Because many fewer people in their 20s have been getting married, there are now many more people in their early 30s who are free to marry,' he said.

Despite the figures, the number of church weddings is in steep decline. They now account for only two out of five weddings – in 1991 religious ceremonies made up just over half. Since 1994 when weddings in 'approved premises' were first permitted, couples have been steadily deserting traditionally dowdy register officers for new and more glamorous surroundings.

Just over half of 'approved premises' weddings are held in hotels, with stately homes, arts venues, museums, and sports facilities such as football grounds also rating high.

While couples marrying for the first time choose 'approved premises', second-timers tend to stick to more low-key register office ceremonies. However, seven per cent of second marriages are celebrated in church or in a religious ceremony – despite the Church of England's official ban on remarriage.

It can be arranged

By Janine Lloyd-Altius

Do you agree or disagree? 'With what?' You're asking. How can you decide unless you've been given some facts to have an opinion on?

Many teenagers from cultures which practise arranged marriages are placed in a similar dilemma. They're asked and sometimes even forced to decide about marrying someone they may not even have met!

Arranged marriages involve the joining of two people by their families. This method is practised by some Buddhists, Orthodox Jews, Sikhs, Muslims, Hindus and a few Christian groups.

Maryam (name changed), a Sikh from Hackney, dreads the arrival of her 16th birthday because she is to be 'married off' by her parents. This won't be the first 'marriage' ordeal Maryam has been subjected to. A previous attempt to present her with a husband has left Maryam, then only 14, with bad experiences. She doesn't want to go through that again.

'I plan to run away when I'm 16,' says Maryam. 'Disappear for good!'

Maryam is one of many teenagers under this marital pressure. Some feel that they will make their parents happy and uphold the family name by consenting.

'I have to agree with arranged marriages because my parents will feel betrayed if I don't,' said one 14-year-old Muslim girl from Hackney.

But youngsters aren't the only ones under pressure. Parents may themselves not agree with this practice but go through with it because they fear disapproval from and loss of status in their community. Who do parents stay true to, their children or their culture? It's an impossible situation.

In all religions, marriage is a sacred ceremony so parents and families feel they need to be involved. Many of the young people *Exposure* interviewed felt that they had to have an arranged marriage for religious reasons:

'I know that I would feel like I had sinned if I don't go through with an arranged marriage,' explained a 16-year-old Muslim girl from Tottenham.

They say the best things in life are free. But with arranged marriages 'love' can be costly in more ways than one. In Islam a 'bride price' is paid by the groom for his wife. So is she a bride or a possession?

Some Sikh families marrying off their daughter feel they need to offer a dowry to attract a worthy groom. Many are burdened with long-term debt as a result. In many cultures the groom's 'potential earning ability' is seen as vital to parents to ensure their daughter's security.

> ### In multi-cultural London it can be difficult to find a partner with the same culture as you. With an arranged marriage, you're guaranteed to be with someone with your traditions

'Money plays a big part in finding a "perfect" partner. Many parents are greedy and go for someone who comes from a wealthy background. I know my dad would!' said Suckhwant, a 14-year-old Muslim girl from Stamford Hill.

Arranged marriages may not be all bad. Many of us go out on the town to check out the talent. But who knows what kind of person you're going to meet in a club, disco or raves full of strangers?

Undoubtedly, our parents know our characters best. They know what we like with our toast in the morning, what song we like to sing in the shower. So aren't parents in a good position to make decisions about who we should marry? If they want the best for us won't they choose the best?

Culture is very important when finding a life partner. If both you and your other half share the same background and values there is a higher chance of you being compatible and your relationship working.

In multi-cultural London it can be difficult to find a partner with the same culture as you. With an arranged marriage, you're guaranteed to be with someone with your traditions. You may not like your chosen partner at first but, by trusting in your parents' judgement, love and friendship can develop.

'Because of the communal and family involvement, marriages are successful and hence divorce rates lower,' believes Mr Britton, a teacher of religious studies at a local secondary school. 'When a marriage takes place, it isn't just a marriage between two people, it is a marriage between two families.'

Kadir, a practising Muslim, explained that a get-out option is always there:

'The girl has the first choice of whether she wants to marry a boy. She has the final word.'

Some agree with arranged marriages and choose to be married this way. They believe it can save the hassle and heartache of finding a husband or wife. Many disagree with arranged marriages but aren't they just imposing their own western values? What's worse?

So, now that *Exposure*'s given you some of the facts, you can develop an opinion and decide for yourself.

• The above article is from *Exposure* Magazine. Their web site can be found at www.exposure.org.uk

Court annuls arranged marriage

By Kirsty Scott

A teenage bride has had her arranged marriage annulled in a rare legal move after a judge ruled she had been 'deceived and frightened' into marrying.

Aneeka Sohrab, from Glasgow, was a 16-year-old schoolgirl when she was forced to marry Raja Khan, a 19-year-old student who had arrived in the UK from Pakistan three months before the wedding in a Glasgow mosque in December 1998.

Miss Sohrab, 19, from the Pollokshields area of Glasgow, had told the court of session in Edinburgh that she was informed of the wedding the week before it was to take place and refused to go through with it.

She said her parents had met Mr Khan's parents in Bury in Lancashire and had agreed that the pair should marry. When she rebelled, she said she was told she would bring disgrace to her family and would have to be sent to Pakistan. Her mother also threatened suicide. The marriage broke down and Miss Sohrab left her husband within months of the wedding. She had asked the court to rule that the marriage was not valid because she had been put under duress. Mr Khan, who had contested the action, claimed Miss Sohrab had been happy to go through with the wedding.

In his written judgment yesterday, the judge, Lord McEwan, granted an order annulling the 'pretended marriage'.

> **'These mothers were of a different generation and were both themselves in arranged marriages,' he said. 'No doubt they thought they were doing the best for their children'**

He said he was satisfied that Miss Sohrab's will had been broken and the pressure put on her to agree to the union was more than a 16-year-old girl could bear. Lord McEwan said it had been clear from a video of the wedding ceremony shown to the court that Miss Sohrab was distressed at the proceedings. 'In spite of her glorious robes she looked a very unhappy girl,' the judge said. Miss Sohrab had told the court she was 'silently protesting' throughout the ceremony.

Lord McEwan said he was very sorry for both the bride and groom and feared their lives had been blighted by the experience. He said both had been dominated by their parents, especially their mothers, and the threat of Miss Sohrab's mother to commit suicide was enough to force her to wed.

'These mothers were of a different generation and were both themselves in arranged marriages,' he said. 'No doubt they thought they were doing the best for their children.

'However, what they both did was put an intolerable pressure on both of these young people at an age when neither was able to take an informed decision about their future or act in any way independently.

'It may be that in the multicultural society in which we now live such situations will continue to arise where ancient ethics clash with the spirit of 21st-century children of a new generation and western ideas, language and what these days passes for culture. There is inevitable tension, and clashes will happen.'

After the court decision, Miss Sohrab's solicitor, Carolyn Mac-Bride, issued a statement on behalf of her client.

'Miss Sohrab is very relieved at the decision,' said Miss MacBride. 'She is happy this allows her to move on with her life. She does not intend to make further comment.'

Bashir Maan, the Scottish representative on the Muslim Council of Great Britain, said: 'If it hasn't been working and one of the parties isn't happy, there's no harm in annulling the marriage. The shariah (Islamic law) does not force the parties to live together. It tells them that the best thing is to try to get on and make up or get the help of a third party, the parents of both sides.'

Divorce and separation

Information from youthinformation.com by the National Youth Agency

Divorce and separation are on the increase. It looks likely that more than a third of all new marriages will end within 20 years and four out of ten of them will end ultimately in divorce. Current trends show that one in four children will experience parental separation or divorce by the age of 16.

What you can expect if your parents are divorcing

If your parents are going through divorce or separation, one of the most important things for them to decide is what arrangements will be made on your behalf. They will decide where you live and with whom. They will also make arrangements for how often you will be able to see the other parent.

If the parents can agree between themselves and with their children where you will live, who you will stay with and how often you can visit the other parent, then there will be no need for you to go to court. This was one of the recommendations set out in the 1989 Children Act.

However, if they cannot decide, the matter is likely to go before the court which can make decisions (known as orders) on behalf of the family. The court's main concern is the welfare of the child involved, not the wishes of your parents. For example:

- a residence order sets out who the children should live with (this can be with one parent or sharing time between both);
- a contact order can allow the children to visit or stay overnight with the parent you don't normally stay with;
- a specific issue order allows one or both parents to make a decision about the children's upbringing (such as the school they go to or whether or not they should receive medical treatment);

- a prohibited steps order prevents parents from doing certain things without first getting permission from the court (for example going on holiday abroad or changing the child's name).

Under the 1989 Children Act the court must make decisions which are in the child's best interest. It must also make the decision as quickly as possible.

Older children and young people should be consulted by the court during divorce proceedings. The court may ask a Court Welfare Officer to come and talk to you and to others who know you (like your teacher). The welfare officer will try to find out what you want and then make recommendations which are in your interest to the court. So it is better to say who you want to live with and what your feelings are about the divorce rather than what you think your parents would like you to say.

Family break-up can be very difficult to handle. It is a time of great uncertainty and upheaval and as a young person you are more than likely to be in the middle of both parents and with confused feelings about them both.

What happens after the divorce is agreed?

The divorce proceedings may be difficult for you but the immediate

unhappiness usually fades with time and most young people are able to settle into a new routine. It will be helpful to you if your parents are able to discuss the separation with you, about what happened in their relationship and why it ended. This will help you come to terms with your change in circumstances.

Helping children cope with divorce

There is a very useful leaflet called *Keeping in touch* which looks at the ways in which children and young people are affected by divorce or separation and offers advice on how parents can help them cope. The leaflet is available free or you can view it on the internet at www.offsol.demon.co.uk

What happens if you are the subject of court proceedings?

Sometimes when there are disagreements between adults during a divorce, the court may have to decide on your future and, by law, must take into account your views and wishes. Young people under the age of 18 will be given a Guardian Ad Litem. This is the legal name given to your Official Solicitor who will put forward your views and wishes during a court hearing.

What is a Ward of Court?

This is a young person under the age of 18 who is protected by the High Court. Someone is only made a Ward of Court under special circumstances. The court will decide where you will live and with whom.

- The above information is from www.youthinformation.com which is run by the National Youth Agency. See page 41 for their address details.

© 2002 National Youth Agency

Broken hearts

Family decline and the consequences for society

The family is the heart of society. If the family fails, society breaks up. Yet family stability has been in remorseless decline over the last 30 years. At the beginning of National Marriage Week, Jill Kirby presents the evidence of child neglect and social disintegration in *Broken Hearts – Family decline and the consequences for society*, published by the Centre for Policy Studies.

Today in Britain there are more children born outside marriage, more teenage pregnancies and more children in poverty than at any time in our history. Britain has the highest divorce rate in Europe, the highest proportion of teenage pregnancies in Europe, and the highest proportion of lone parents in Europe.

Recent moves to reduce the distinction between marriage and cohabitation ignore the evidence. The children of both lone and cohabiting parents are more likely to suffer physical abuse than the children of married couples; to experience mental breakdown; to turn to drugs; to commit crime; and to run away from home. And a cohabiting couple is far less likely to remain together after the birth of a child than a married couple.

Government efforts to tackle child poverty are dealing only with symptoms, not causes. Where the state intervenes to replace family support, it provides greater incentives not to marry.

It need not be like this. Most other European economies have fiscal instruments of support for marriage, through joint taxation. In Britain, family commitments have become largely irrelevant to tax assessment, whereas in most of Europe adults with families to support are paying tax at much lower rates than single earners.

For the sake of the children and to repair the damage to society, it is time for the state to signal its approbation and support for the structure most successful in maintaining social stability: the married family.

Jill Kirby throws down a challenge to today's politicians and opinion-formers: first, to openly acknowledge the link between family stability and a strong and peaceful society and second, to implement policies which will turn the tide.

Today in Britain there are more children born outside marriage, more teenage pregnancies and more children in poverty than at any time in our history

---

'Unless we are prepared to recognise that the family is under siege and that marriage is under threat, we can have no hope of reversing the trend and improving the lives of the children who are afflicted.'

In the author's words: 'The nurture of children should be a primary objective of every civilised society. The perverse consequence of our fiscal, social and welfare policies has been to incentivise and institutionalise child neglect. It is time for a new approach.'

• Broken Hearts – *family decline and the consequence for society*, published February 2002, by the Centre for Policy Studies, 57 Tufton Street, London SWIP 3QL. Price £7.50. See page 41 for their address details.

© *Centre for Policy Studies*

Age at first marriage

The table below shows an EU comparison of the average age at first marriage, by gender for 1961 and 1998.

	1961		1998	
	Males	Females	Males	Females
Denmark	25.7	22.8	31.7	29.4
Sweden	26.6	23.8	31.7	29.3
Greece	29.2	25.2	30.3	26.5
Italy	28.5	24.7	30.0	27.1
Irish Republic	30.8	27.6	30.0	28.2
Netherlands	26.4	24.1	30.0	27.6
Germany	25.4	23.4	29.5	26.9
Finland	25.8	23.6	29.5	27.5
France	25.6	23.0	29.6	27.6
Spain	28.8	26.1	29.4	27.4
Luxembourg[1]	26.9	25.4	29.6	27.2
Austria	26.5	23.8	29.2	26.7
England and Wales	25.6	23.1	29.1	27.0
Belgium	25.0	22.8	27.8	25.7
Portugal	26.9	24.8	27.1	25.1
EU average	**26.7**	**24.1**	**29.6**	**27.3**

The average age at first marriage in the EU as a whole in 1998 was around three years higher than in 1961: 30 for men and 27 for women in 1998, compared with 27 and 24 in 1961.

1 Data are for 1990 not 1998

Source: Social Trends 32, Crown copyright

The cost of family breakdown

Executive summary

The family in Britain is in crisis. This is acknowledged by commentators across the political and social spectrum. Family breakdown is widespread. Few people do not know someone whose family has been affected by separation, divorce, cohabitation or single parenthood. There were 145,000 divorces in Britain in 1998, affecting just over 150,000 children. Each failed relationship produces pain and emotional hurt, creating an incalculable cost in human misery. The whole of society is affected by the social consequences of family breakdown. Huge financial costs are incurred not only by the individuals concerned, but also by local communities, the taxpayer, and society at large. Family breakdown impairs the health of the nation, reduces the educational achievement of its children, increases the crime rate, places a burden on the national economy and a strain on social relationships at all levels.

Earlier research has quantified the costs of family breakdown in the range £4 billion to £10 billion. This report concludes that these previous estimates significantly understate the actual cost of family breakdown, and estimates that the direct annual costs are nearer to £15 billion, and rising. With indirect costs, the total is much more, quite possibly double that. The direct costs of family breakdown cost each of the UK's 26.2 million tax payers an average of £11 per week. Direct costs of £15 billion equate with about one-third of government expenditure on education, just over a quarter of what it spends on the NHS, or almost exactly the combined totals it spends on industry, agriculture and employment, or on housing and the environment. Public money spent tackling the social problems caused by family breakdown could otherwise fund creative social projects which strengthen family life and national unity.

Some of the costs of family breakdown are readily identifiable. The largest is the cost of welfare support and payments for children and parents, amounting to £8.5 billion. There are other less obvious costs, such as Legal Aid; the running costs of the Child Support Agency, special needs schools (disproportionately used by children from broken families), and child psychology services; some of the costs of the criminal justice system, remand centres and prisons; plus additional costs of health due to family breakdown. These can be estimated. Quantifying the lost potential as a result of family breakdown is infinitely more difficult.

As a generalisation, the likelihood of adverse outcomes for children from broken families is about twice that from intact families. These children start out in life with a huge man-made handicap. Children whose parents have divorced or whose cohabitation relationship has broken down are increasingly the victims of abuse and neglect. The rate of sexual abuse of girls by their stepfathers is at least six times higher than for girls in intact families by their biological parents.

Children from broken homes exhibit more health, emotional and behavioural problems; they have higher rates of suicide; and they are more frequently involved in drug abuse and crime, and have higher rates of suicide. Half of young offenders come from broken homes. They also perform badly at school, are less likely to go on to further education and more likely to get low-paid jobs. They are twice as likely to suffer divorce or relationship breakdown in adult life than children from intact families.

While the report's authors believe that marriage has proven through the ages to provide the surest foundations for a stable society and for raising children, the purpose of this report is not to moralise. Our principal purpose is to alert Parliament and the British people to the serious state of affairs which prevails in family life. In particular, we challenge those who are indifferent to, or even contemptuous of, 'family values' to acknowledge the massive financial and social costs which society at large is paying – costs which show no sign of diminishing.

If the current trend is to be reversed, many agencies will need to be involved. The churches need to give a clear, unambiguous lead. Government must acknowledge its duty to guide, lead and set the tone. Rather than sit on the fence,

government must be prepared to discriminate positively in favour of marriage as an ideal. This report makes a number of recommendations, many of which could be implemented by the government. But ultimately the state of the family in Britain will not improve unless people themselves desire change. A first step towards strengthening family life and protecting children has to be the recognition of the effects of family breakdown, its cost, both financially and in human suffering. What is needed above all is a cultural change at grass-roots level, which acknowledges that the traditional family is the very foundation of a stable, prosperous and caring society.

• The above information is an extract from the Family Matters Institute's web site which can be found at www.the-park.net/familymatters/index.html

Children and divorce

Information from Divorce-Online Limited

One out of every two marriages today ends in divorce and many divorcing families include children. Parents who are getting a divorce are frequently worried about the effect the divorce will have on their children. During this difficult period, parents may be preoccupied with their own problems, but continue to be the most important people in their children's lives.

While parents may be devastated or relieved by the divorce, children are invariably frightened and confused by the threat to their security. Some parents feel so hurt or overwhelmed by the divorce that they may turn to the child for comfort or direction. Children can misinterpret divorce unless parents tell them what is happening, how they are involved and not involved and what will happen to them.

Children often believe they have caused the conflict between their mother and father. Many children assume the responsibility for bringing their parents back together, sometimes by sacrificing themselves. Vulnerability to both physical and mental illnesses can originate in the traumatic loss of one or both parents through divorce. With care and attention, however, a family's strengths can be mobilised during a divorce, and children can be helped to deal constructively with the resolution of parental conflict.

Parents should be alert to signs of distress in their child or children. Young children may react to divorce by becoming more aggressive and

uncooperative or withdrawing. Older children may feel deep sadness and loss. Their schoolwork may suffer and behaviour problems are common. As teenagers and adults, children of divorce often have trouble with their own relationships and experience problems with self-esteem.

Children will do best if they know that their mother and father will still be their parents and remain involved with them even though the marriage is ending and the parents won't live together. Long custody disputes or pressure on a child to 'choose sides' can be particularly harmful for the youngster and can add to the damage of the divorce. Research shows that children do best when parents can co-operate on behalf of the child.

It is always good to keep a record of any problems that arise in case you have to go to court.

If you need to make an application to the court for residence (custody) or contact (access) use our Children Act LegalPac to save hundreds of pounds on legal fees.

While parents may be devastated or relieved by the divorce, children are invariably frightened and confused by the threat to their security

• The above information is an extract from Divorce-Online News, April 2002, from the web site www.divorce-online.co.uk

D-I-V-O-R-C-E

Every parent worries, but an American academic says research shows the vast majority of offspring suffer no long-term damage from a collapsed marriage

'My friends are always talking about their mummies and daddies and wedding anniversaries,' complains 13-year-old Fiona from Belfast. 'Christmas is hard because everyone talks about having a big family dinner. To hear stuff like that really hurts. I sometimes get really angry with my parents for getting divorced. I'd give my last breath to have them back together.'

Nothing triggers guilt in a parent more chillingly than the fear that their divorce might damage a child for life. If Fiona is angry now, could she become sicker, less well educated, disturbed or simply unhappier in adulthood as a consequence of her childhood bad luck? For a generation, parents worldwide have been desperate to know whether they are doing what they cannot bear to contemplate – irrevocably damaging those they brought into the world.

But this week a major new US study is bringing reassurance to millions worldwide. Research over 25 years suggests that the vast majority of children whose parents divorce suffer no long-term damage at all. The news has sparked a furious row on the other side of the Atlantic and the fallout will almost certainly soon be felt here.

E. Mavis Hetherington is professor emeritus at the University of Virginia. A distinguished psychologist, she is touring her home country this weekend to relieved acclaim from babyboomers, the generation for whom divorce became acceptable. But she is easily able to brush aside charges from detractors that she is merely one of the 'Bohemian elite', fluffy promoters of liberal values based on touchy-feely sociology.

First, Hetherington hardly fits the classic liberal stereotype. Married for 46 years with three apparently stable children, she says: 'I harbour no doubts about the ability of divorce to devastate. It can and does ruin

By Ben Summerskill and Ed Vulliamy, The Observer

lives. But, that said, I also think that much writing on divorce – popular and academic – has exaggerated its negative effects and ignored its sometimes considerable positive effects.

'Love is not enough,' Hetherington told *The Observer*. 'Help and care for these children has to be disciplined as well. After all you've put them through, it can't be harsh. But if things are organised and both parents accept the challenges together, they can help children through the difficult times with great success.'

Hetherington's second bulwark against criticism is the very extent of the analysis in her best-selling *For Better or Worse: Divorce Reconsidered*. All too little research covers the development of children throughout childhood. Ask an adult why they are disturbed and they often attribute their state, criminality or ill-health to divorced parents.

Almost four out of five children of divorce function well, with little long-term damage

But by tracking 2,500 people in 1,400 families from childhood, Hetherington has been able to analyse not just outcome but exact cause. Her archive includes not only statistical information but tens of thousands of hours of 'secret' videotape of families at dinner, relaxing or fighting their ways through trauma and rows.

Hetherington concludes that almost four out of five children of divorce function well, with little long-term damage. Within two years, the vast majority are beginning to 'function reasonably well'. Perhaps

just as important, 70 per cent of divorced parents are happier afterwards than they were before.

Inevitably, the new research has rattled the cages of both political and religious champions of the sanctity of marriage. Two years ago, retired Californian professor Judith Wallerstein created another American publishing sensation with a supposedly seminal work claiming that the damage of divorce to children was deep and long-term, making them unable to develop proper relations in later life.

Wallerstein is a leading member of the ideologically conservative American Society of Family Values. Her research, Hetherington is only too happy to retort, 'was based on couples who had psychological problems anyway. What's more, she was doing it in Marin County [a famously rich suburb of San Francisco] where there is a high divorce rate.'

But above all, Hetherington offers the defence that her latest conclusions are certainly not unremittingly rosy. She admits that 25 per cent of children from divorced families have serious emotional or social problems of some sort. That compares with 10 per cent from those families that stay together. So there is still an acknowledgement that risks from divorce exist, but are nowhere near as awful as many once feared.

For Better or Worse also features the same grim, traditional patterns as elsewhere: young boys who rebel against their mothers, girls who are sexually precocious at an early age, a higher proportion of children of divorcees getting divorced themselves.

'I've never seen a victimless divorce,' Hetherington admits. 'But a lot of the current work makes it sound as if you've given your kids a terminal disease when they go through a divorce. One of the reasons I wanted to write this book was not only to get the figures out, but to say that if we put children through this then tell them they are never going to recover, this is damaging in itself. A child is going to spend its grown-up life thinking: "When are these terrible things going to happen to me?"'

British parents have also been bombarded for decades with research – some tendentious, some apparently reliable – suggesting that children from divorced households may do less well in later life than their counterparts. But all too often the information is viewed through a prism that is acceptable to those who present it.

The *Daily Mail*, with its traditional 'family values' agenda, is happy to remind parents that 'couples who marry stay together' and that is good for children. That, on the surface, is true. An average marriage lasts nine years. An average cohabitation less than three. But figures are what you make them. People who cohabit might not marry precisely because they do not view their relationship as long-term and want to wait for one that will be. The same approach is taken all too often to data about children as well.

Last year, Professor Bob Rowthorn from Cambridge University joined the divorce debate, to furious reaction. A former communist, he announced that he had ditched his former belief in 'lifestyle choice' and now supported marriage. 'The traditional view was usually right,' he claimed. 'The scientific evidence in favour of marriage is overwhelming.'

Rowthorn was attacked as a 'mere economist' – which he is. But detractors on that count ignore all too easily the fact that for many broken families, the division of household income in two can lead to

crisis. Poverty is a far more certain indicator of poor school performance and ill health than divorce itself. But that is a persuasive argument for a fairer split of household assets, rather than – necessarily – a denunciation of divorce.

'We just need to accept that divorce is a reasonable solution to an unhappy, acrimonious, destructive marital relationship'

There also remains a vocal minority opposed to divorce for religious reasons. Colin Hart, director of the Christian Institute, said: 'Nobody's saying that every child whose parents divorce experiences all the negative consequences, but many do. Frankly, I thought these arguments were settled long ago.'

The debate will become heated again as protagonists argue about the Civil Partnership Bill currently being considered by the House of Lords. Is this 'marriage lite', a sop to cohabitees which will make it easier for them to leave each other and their children? Or will it promote serious relationships among those who don't want the formal baggage of traditional marriage forced on them?

Between the flak, the bridge Hetherington's latest research might help us all to cross is that between the world as some would like to see it and the world as it is. Almost four in 10 marriages still end in divorce and the latest British Social Attitudes Survey found that two-thirds of 18- to 24-year-olds no longer believe

people should get married before having children.

Lisa Harker, deputy director of the Institute for Public Policy Research and a family expert, said: 'For too long, there has been a lot of emotion in this debate. What has been lacking is a cool-headed, thorough piece of research over a long period of time. That is why Hetherington's work is a welcome contribution.

'For many years, there has been a growing body of evidence suggesting that it is not divorce *per se* that has a detrimental effect upon children. It is the way that the divorce process is handled.'

And Maryly La Follette, a leading London divorce lawyer, said: 'It would be instructive to track the 80 per cent of children in this research who have not suffered from divorce and establish if it was their parents who were able to resolve disputes by agreement, with no attempts to hamper contact between the children and the non-resident parent. That is often a key ingredient in how children are affected. Separation can be resolved amicably if people put their minds to it. Look at the case of Kate Winslet and Jim Threapleton earlier this year.'

But in both the UK and America what still infuriates Hetherington, just as it does her British counterparts, is the notion that they are for one moment 'pro-divorce'.

'Mine is anything but a pro-divorce book, but it's a pro-good marriage book,' the psychologist says. 'I hope it will help people to cope with the changes in their lives and give them strength in coping. We just need to accept that divorce is a reasonable solution to an unhappy, acrimonious, destructive marital relationship.'

Thirteen-year-old Erin from Sheffield admits: 'All things considered, I'm glad my parents are divorced. It's impossible to imagine them together and I wouldn't want it to be that way. Divorce will always affect children. The key thing is how you let it affect you.'

• Comments from young people come from *Children's Express*, a programme of learning through journalism for young people aged eight to 18.

© Guardian Newspapers Limited 2002

Helping children cope with divorce

Innovative web site launched to help children cope with divorce

NCH is launching a brand new web site. The web site, funded by the Lord Chancellor's Department, is the very first on-line resource designed to give information and support to children whose parents are divorcing or separating. Children's BBC TV presenter Adrian Dickson and B*witched singer Keavy Lynch will be joining Rosie Winterton MP, Parliamentary Secretary to the Lord Chancellor's Department, at midday in the Children's Section of St Pancras Library in London to be the first people to log on to the web site.

NCH believes that the need for a resource to inform and support children and young people experiencing family breakdown is clear. The UK still has the highest divorce rate in Europe. In 2000 the parents of more than 142,000 UK children under the age of 16 got divorced. Many thousands more experienced their parents' separation. Years of experience of working with children and parents in this situation have taught NCH that when parents split up it's usually the children who have the least access to information – at the time when they want and need it the most.

www.itsnotyourfault.org will give children and young people of all ages, and their parents, access to a range of useful information to help them to find ways to adjust to their new family life. Young net surfers will be introduced to friendly icon Patch the Dog who will guide them through the range of emotions they may be feeling, like anger, sadness, confusion and guilt. Expert advice is featured alongside other children sharing their stories. The web site also points both children and parents in the direction of other services designed to help the whole family. NCH hopes that this initiative will reach every child in the UK that

needs it, via home, school or library Internet access.

NCH is the largest single provider of family mediation and related child-counselling services in the UK. Vicky Leach, NCH's Family Mediation adviser, says:

The UK still has the highest divorce rate in Europe. In 2000 the parents of more than 142,000 UK children under the age of 16 got divorced

---

'Children sometimes tell us that their parents' decision to separate feels like the end of the world. Others know it's the right thing and accept it. Whatever the individual circumstance most parents find it hard to talk to their children about what is happening while they are splitting up. What all children have in common is the need for information, the need to know that they're not

the only one to be going through this and the need to know that things will get better.

'www.itsnotyourfault.org aims to provide a first port of call for all children whose parents are divorcing or separating. For some it will answer practical questions about what is happening and the legal process, for others it will be the first step in dealing with their emotions. NCH hopes that for all of them it will demonstrate that they aren't to blame and that divorce is not the end of the world.'

NCH consulted with children and young people on the content of the web-site as it was being created. 14-year-old David says:

'My parents split up when I was 6 years old. Having Internet access and a web site like this would have been really useful. I like the way the web site shows that the split-up between adults is not the child's fault – this is the way adults should explain things to children!'

• The above information is an extract from NCH's web site which can be found at www.nch.org.uk

My family's changing

Information from the Lord Chancellor's Department

There are lots of reasons why relationships don't always work out and parents decide to split up, but it is usually because one or both of them is unhappy and they believe that they need to be apart for things to get better.

Lots of children's families change when their parents split up.

Here are some of the most common reasons:

- Growing or drifting apart.
- Wanting different things.
- Not being able to spend much time together.
- Wanting to be with someone else.
- Having lots of disagreements.

The reasons are different for every family.

Always remember:
It's not your fault that this is happening

Your Mum and Dad will always be your parents even if they are not together any more.

Is my family normal?

'I sometimes get jealous of my friends because I think they've got a normal life still, with just a Mum and Dad.'
Ellie, age 14

But what is normal?
Families come in all sorts of shapes and sizes . . .

'I live with my Mum in the week and with my Nan on Friday and Saturday nights.'
Tanika, age 8

'Me and my brother live with my Dad and his girlfriend and her three children.'
Lenny, age 10

'I live with a family who look after me, and sometimes I see my Mum.'
Kelly, age 12

'I visit my Dad every other weekend.'
Ellie, age 14

'My Mum and Dad split up when I was a baby but I spend the same amount of time at both their houses.'
Jade, age 11

'My Mum died when I was little so it's just me and my Dad.'
Sophia, age 10

. . . so, there's really no such thing as a normal family.

Change is not always easy, especially if lots of people are involved. It might take some time for everyone to get used to new or different ways.

Facts at your fingertips

- About one out of every four children has parents who get divorced.
- About 650 children see their parents separate or get divorced every day.
- 1.5 million children visit a parent at the weekends or during the holidays.
- Over 2.5 million children are now growing up as part of a stepfamily.
- About 300,000 children have parents who have been married to other people before.

What happens when parents divorce?

A marriage can only be ended by an order from the County Court. A County Court is a court for your local area, and is very different from the courts that deal with crime.

Usually, it is not necessary for anyone to actually go to the court for a divorce as things can usually be dealt with by post.

Your parents may talk to mediators (people who are trained in helping parents to come to

Marriages and divorces

The number of first marriages peaked in 1970 at almost 390 thousand, and since has decreased to less than half this number – 179 thousand in 1999.

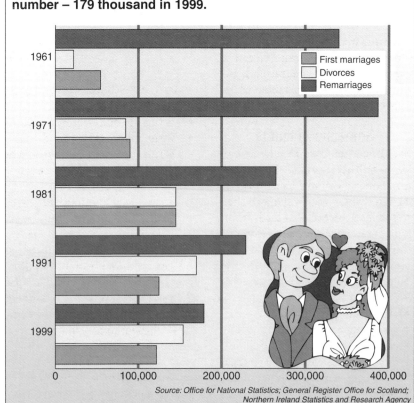

Source: Office for National Statistics; General Register Office for Scotland; Northern Ireland Statistics and Research Agency

agreements) or get advice from lawyers (specialists on the law) about how best to agree future plans – things like money, where people are going to live and, most importantly, arrangements for you.

Sometimes parents find it too difficult to agree on future arrangements and so a judge can make decisions for them. These are known as Court Orders.

The judge may be asked to make decisions about residence (who you live with) or contact (the arrangements for having contact with the parent who doesn't live with you any more).

To do this, they may ask a Children and Family Reporter from the Children and Family Court Advisory and Support Service to talk to you and your parents and then give advice to the court on the best arrangements.

When the judge has all the information to make a decision, a Court Hearing may be arranged to discuss the arrangements. A Court Hearing is a meeting between the judge and your parents to hear what everyone has to say. Children are not usually called to the court because it's the job of the Children and Family Reporter to make sure that the children's views are passed on to the judge.

It can be really hard and upsetting when your parents split up. However, most children find that in time, things do get better and they can eventually feel okay about what's happened.

Someone to talk to

We all need someone to talk to. Don't keep things bottled up inside, especially if you are going through big family changes. You may be able to talk to your Mum or Dad. If not, here are some other people you may feel able to speak to. Make sure it is someone you trust.
- a grandparent
- a sister or brother
- a cousin
- an aunt or uncle
- a friend
- someone you know who has been through a similar thing
- a teacher at school
- a friend's Mum

- a youth worker or play worker
- a counsellor (someone whose job it is to listen to how you feel)

If you don't want to talk to someone you know, you could call one of the numbers at the end of the article.

I'm angry

If you are angry, sad or worried it is quite normal to want to be quiet and not want to talk. But sometimes bottled-up feelings can make you feel a bit sick, like you have butterflies in your stomach, or they can stop you sleeping because you are worried.

Here's how to let out some of those bottled-up feelings:
- Talk to someone.
- Do something that makes you happy: see a film, re-read a favourite book, or listen to your favourite music.
- Paint a picture (really big). Use loads of paint and bright colours to show how you feel. You could try red for anger, blue for calm and happy, yellow for nervous, purple for sad, and green for jealous.
- Write in your (secret) diary.
- Write a letter to a friend.
- Write a letter to the person who is making you feel bad but rip it up before you send it.
- Sport – playing football, swimming, dancing or just running fast can all make you feel better.
- If you feel really mad, hit a big, soft cushion or yell into a pillow.

None of these things will solve all your problems or make things go back to just the way they were, but some of them may help.

So what is a lone-parent family?

A lone-parent family is when you live with only one of your parents,

your Mum or your Dad. You may sometimes see or stay with your other parent, you may have no contact, or your other parent may have died.

So what is a stepfamily?

A stepfamily is when one or both of your parents are in a relationship with someone who isn't your Mum or Dad (like your Mum or Dad's boyfriend or girlfriend, or your Mum or Dad's new husband or wife) who may have children, too. Some people feel happy to use the word 'stepfamily', others don't like it. Whatever you choose, it's okay.

Getting along

You don't like your Mum's boyfriend, or you and his children just don't get on. You know you're stuck with them even though you wish you weren't. What can you do?

Help tips
- Keep busy. Being with your friends and doing something you really like can help you get through tough times.
- Always be yourself. Don't try to change the way you are to please other people. Take time to get to know them. You may find you like some of the same things.
- Think of at least one good thing about each person.
- Try to think about things from the other person's point of view. If your stepsister is really whingey, or your stepbrother locks himself in his room all evening, perhaps they're unhappy about being part of a new family, too.
- Remember, you don't have to love everyone, but in time you may end up liking them.

Sharing your space
You may have to get used to living with new people. What's it like?

'At first, it was a nightmare having to live with them when you didn't even know them.'
Charlotte, age 12

'Although I'm not at my Dad's all the time, I feel at home because I keep my own stuff there.'
Emma, age 14

'They have rules that you don't understand or are not used to.'
Sian, age 14

Tips

Keep some of your favourite things around you to make you feel happier.

Don't feel you have to get rid of any things even if they make your Mum or Dad upset. Explain to them that they make YOU feel better.

If you can't have your own room, make sure you have a space to keep your own things.

It's all in a name

Imagine your Mum or Dad has a new boyfriend or girlfriend. Perhaps your Mum or Dad is getting remarried or maybe your Mum or Dad's new husband or wife and kids are going to come and live with you. What do you call them? And how do you describe them to your friends?

'I call my Mum's boyfriend Uncle Sylvester. I know he's not my real Uncle or anything but we like it.'
Jamal, age 6

'It winds me up when my stepsister calls my Dad, Dad. He's my Dad, not hers.'
Leon, age 9

'I call Winston by his name. Although he's like a father figure, he's not my Dad.'
Matt, age 15

'I wanted to have the same surname as my Mum, stepdad and step-brother. It's great now it's changed because I'm higher up on the register.'
Ellie, age 14

Words from the wise

. . . about feelings

'It's not your fault.'
Andy, age 11

'Make sure you don't blame yourself for the break-up.'
Philip, age 9

'Remember, your feelings are important and normal.'
Kelly, age 12

'Talk to someone and let them know how you are feeling. Don't let it eat away at you on the inside.'
Flora, age 14

. . . about new families

'It can get better . . . there are less arguments now than when my parents were together.'
Brita, age 13

'Your parents don't love you any less.'
Sian, age 14

'You have more people to talk to and be with. There are more people to care about you.'
Luke, age 7

'Just try to give them a chance.'
Anthony, age 8

Getting help

ChildLine: 0800 1111
(Freephone 24 hours a day)
www.childline.org.uk
Special help line for children. Call for free advice or just someone to talk to.

Children's Legal Centre
01206 873 820
(10.00-12.30pm, 2-4.30pm week days) information on the law for children.

Youth Access
020 8772 9900
(9.30 am–5.30 pm Monday to Friday) Will tell you where you can go for help in your local area.

Parentline Plus
www.parentlineplus.org.uk
Information for young people freephone helpline for parents: 0808 800 2222.

NSPCC
Helpline 0808 800 5000
(Freephone 24 hours a day)
Offers counselling, information and advice for anyone concerned about a child at risk of abuse, including children themselves.

Who Cares?
Linkline 0500 564 570
(Freephone 3.30-6.00 pm Monday, Wednesday and Thursday). Advice and support if you have been or are in care.

Samaritans
08457 909090
(Freephone 24 hours a day)
Advice and support if you feel really unhappy and depressed.

CRUSE Bereavement Care
020 8332 7227
Help, advice and support if a relative or a friend has died.

National Youth Advocacy Service
0800 616101
Freephone 9am-9pm Monday to Friday 2-8pm weekends information, advice and representation (someone who can speak for you).

© Crown copyright

Family mediation

Information from National Family Mediation (NFM)

Family mediation helps those involved in family breakdown to communicate better with one another and reach their own decisions about all or some of the issues arising from separation or divorce – children, property and finance.

Mediation is about directly negotiating your own decisions with the help of a third party. It is an alternative to solicitors negotiating for you or having decisions made for you by the courts. Entering mediation is always voluntary.

How does mediation work?
A trained mediator will meet with you both for a series of sessions in which you will be helped to

- Identify all the matters you wish to consider
- Collect the necessary information
- Talk about the choices open to you
- Negotiate with each other to reach decisions that are acceptable to you both
- Discuss how you can consult your children appropriately about arrangements

What does the mediator do?
The mediator's job is to act as an impartial third party and manage the process, helping you to exchange information, ideas and feelings constructively and ensuring that you make informed decisions. The mediator has no power to impose a settlement – responsibility for all decisions remains with yourselves since you know better than anyone else what is right for your family. The mediator will not advise you about the best option either for your children or your financial affairs, nor can the mediator protect your individual interest.

Will I still need a solicitor?
Yes. You will need a solicitor to advise you on the personal consequences for you of your proposals. You will be encouraged to engage a solicitor whom you can consult during the mediation process. At the end of mediation your solicitor will be able to advise you about your proposals and translate them into a legally binding form.

Will we have anything in writing?
At the end of mediation you will usually have achieved a written summary of the proposals you have reached. This is not a legally binding document and you will need legal advice about it especially if you have reached agreement on financial and property issues.

How much will it cost?
Each Service has their own scale of charges. They will also be able to advise you if you are eligible for legally aided mediation, which is free.

Is mediation suitable for everybody?
Sometimes mediation is not the best way for you to resolve your problems. You will have a chance to discuss this in more detail at your first individual meeting with the mediator.

Is mediation confidential?
Firstly mediation is *confidential* and courts are also likely to regard the discussions as *privileged*.

Confidentiality – The Service will not voluntarily disclose to outsiders any information obtained in the course of your discussions without first obtaining your permission (unless it appears there is a risk of significant harm to adult or child).

Privilege – What you say during mediation cannot be used later in court as evidence. But facts disclosed during mediation are regarded as open information and although strictly confidential may be used subsequently in court.

Will the mediator talk to the children?
In mediation you are regarded as the experts on your children and will have valuable knowledge and information about their needs, wishes and views. However there may be times when you both would like the mediator to consult directly with the children about your plans. In those circumstances children would be asked for their specific comments and views on your joint proposals, without having to take sides in any difference of opinion between their parents.

Such a meeting needs careful planning and is confidential in so far as the mediator and children agree what the mediator will say to the parents after the meeting.

What are the benefits of mediation?
Research conducted by the Joseph Rowntree Foundation with Newcastle University identified that three years later couples felt that mediation had helped them to

- End the marital relationship amicably
- Reduce conflict
- Maintain good relationships with their ex-spouses
- Carry less bitterness and resentment into their post-divorce lives
- Be more content with existing child care arrangements and less likely to have disagreement about child contact
- Be able to reach agreement that had survived the test of time
- Be glad they had used mediation.

How can I contact a mediator?
If you would like to contact an NFM Service in your area for more information, or to arrange an appointment, please visit our web site at www.nfm.u-net.com, click on the 'Offices' button. The map will help you to find a Service near you.

© *National Family Mediation (NFM)*

> **Mediation is about directly negotiating your own decisions with the help of a third party. Entering mediation is always voluntary**

Stepfamilies

Information from ChildLine

Some facts and figures about the family today

- Recent research indicates that around a half of all divorces will occur within the first ten years of marriage.
- It is now probable that one in four children will experience their parents' divorce before they reach sixteen.
- Currently in Britain there are over 2.5 million children in stepfamily life. One million live in their stepfamily; another million visit their stepfamily.

Children are affected by changes in the family. Many children will live in a variety of family environments during their childhood and adolescence.

Stepfamilies

Stepfamilies come together when people marry again or live with a new partner. This may be after the death of one parent, separation or divorce. It can also mean that children from different families end up living together for all or part of the time.

In 2000/2001 over 15,000 children called ChildLine to talk about their family relationships, many of which concerned stepfamilies. A further 1,525 called about parents divorcing or separating.

Some children are very happy, but for others, coping with stepparents, stepbrothers and stepsisters can be a difficult and lonely experience. Settling into a new family situation can always be difficult for the children involved, but this usually resolves itself with time. However, for other children problems can arise in relation to how well they do at school and their general health and well-being. This can result in depression or children feeling stressed and unhappy. What appears to be most important is that children continue to retain a healthy relationship with both their natural parents.

Children have told ChildLine counsellors:

Michael, 12: *'It's hard getting to know lots of new people all at once.'*

Alison, 15: *'He seems to think he can tell me what to do, but he hasn't got the right. He isn't my real dad.'*

Janine, 13: *'I feel like Mum's a different person.'*

Remi, 13: *'I think that Samuel and his children are more special to her now.'*

Alice, 15: *'It feels wrong when I'm having fun with Dad and his new wife, when I think of Mum by herself.'*

Stef, 13: *'I'm not sure who to go to now, when I want to talk about things.'*

Paula, 10: *'I most want my mum back and for everything to be OK again.'*

Alex, 16: *'Every time I go out with Dad, he quizzes me about Mum and my new step-dad. I feel like a spy.'*

Other worries stepchildren may have

Sometimes stepchildren continue to see both their birth parents, but others may lose touch with one of them. There can be pressure to be a 'perfect family', but it takes time to get to know one another. Just getting used to different ways that each person has can cause problems. Different rules and expectations, kinds of food eaten, when homework is done or what household tasks you

---

Some children are very happy, but for others, coping with stepparents, stepbrothers and stepsisters can be a difficult and lonely experience

---

would be expected to do are all things that cause stress. Family holidays, Christmas and other religious festivals are all times when each family has its own ways of doing things and it can be hard to adjust to new ways.

Children might have to move house, neighbourhood and school. It can mean losing friends and moving away from loved relatives. Families combining can mean less privacy; for example, sharing a bedroom, or never having somewhere quiet to do homework or just be alone. It can be a difficult time for parents too – they are having to be a parent for a child they hardly know.

How ChildLine can help

It can be hard to find someone with the time to listen when so many changes are happening, and children sometimes feel that they are expected to just get on with it. Although a new family situation won't be the same as before, being part of a stepfamily can be very positive and good for the children involved. It's worth remembering that while things can go wrong, there may also be a means by which to put them right.

Young people may need to go through a grieving process, letting old habits, family ceremonies and ways of doing things go by. They can feel a lot of stress, anger and sadness. Talking can help with all these feelings.

ChildLine takes children's and young people's problems seriously, giving them a chance to talk in confidence about their concerns, however large or small. ChildLine counsellors can also tell them where to go for more information, including local sources of help and advice. This service is free and available 24 hours a day, seven days a week. Freephone: 0800 1111 or Freepost 1111, London N1 0BR or ChildLine Minicom: 0800 400 222, Mon-Fri 9.30am-9.30pm, Sat-Sun 9.30am-8.00pm

© ChildLine
January 2002

Divorce, separation, new families

How to help your child through family change

Over 1 in 4 children in Britain will experience the divorce of their parents by the time they are 16 and many more will experience the separation of their parents who are not married. Most of these children's parents will re-marry or re-partner.

The experience of losing the family structure you are familiar with can be distressing, especially for children, and they may grieve for this particularly when one or both of their parents embarks on a new relationship.

Parentline Plus has worked with young people to find out how they experience parental divorce and separation. Many children are able to adjust to the change and also to the formation of a new family with new stepbrothers and sisters, but the adults around them play an important role in helping them to do this. Here are their suggestions of how you can best support them.

Talking

It's not easy to help your child to talk about their feelings: it's hard to hear that they may be unhappy. If feelings are bottled up their mood and

Parentline_{plus}

behaviour can be affected. Your child may not feel able to tell you that they are angry, upset or missing your ex-partner. Nor may they be ready to tell you their true feelings, but try to provide some opportunities for them to talk.

Listening

Your child may want something that is not possible, like you getting back together with your ex-partner. They still need to express their views and have explanations as to why their wishes are not possible. Children who don't feel listened to, feel powerless, which can have a major influence on their feelings of self-worth and their behaviour. Listening lets them know that you care about how they feel and that you want to understand their point of view. It helps them feel valued.

Honesty

You may feel it will be easier on the children if you protect them from the truth. Keeping things from them

makes young people feel that their feelings don't matter. They may fill in the gaps of what they know by imagining scenarios that are worse than reality. In addition, if they do not know why and when their parents are splitting up they may feel they have done something to cause the situation. Let them know they are not to blame.

Stuck in the middle

Don't make young people feel pressured to take sides. They may still have feelings and loyalties for both parents. It will be easier for them to adjust if you co-operate over arrangements and resist prying questions about your ex-partner. Otherwise they may feel used.

Rejection, isolation and being ignored

A child may feel that they have been forgotten if they have less contact with a parent. Whether or not you live with your children just try to set some time aside to talk to them, in person, by letter or phone.

Visiting the parent they don't live with and their new family

Children will need time to adjust to

- IF I KEEP PRESSING THE REWIND BUTTON THINGS WILL GO BACK TO HOW THEY WERE...

- PRESS FAST FORWARD AND YOU'LL SEE WE'RE STILL YOUR PARENTS...

new homes and circumstances, the ways that things are now done and sharing a parent's time. Try to be patient.

Keeping in contact with other relatives

Children need reassurance that not all the adults in their lives are changing. Many young people want to continue seeing their grandparents and other relatives. It helps them feel more secure and that there is some continuity in their family life.

Relationships with step-parents

To your children, your new partner is a stranger and so they will need time to get to know and trust him/her. Try not to rush them into giving your partner affection.

Discipline

Develop a relationship with your partner's children before attempting discipline so that there is some trust and respect between you. You may also find that you and your partner have different ideas about discipline, but try to agree basic rules and involve all the family.

Money

Try to negotiate about arrangements concerning who pays for what, when and how often, without involving the children. Otherwise they can feel used, and/or that they are contributing to the difficulty of the situation.

Presents

Get to know your partner's children before buying them gifts. You may want to show them you care but they may feel you are not genuine or are not making a real effort.

Stepbrothers/sisters

Children and young people are learning how to share their parents with others. Sometimes they may feel that they are not being treated fairly. Try not to take sides.

New house

Children may also be adjusting to a new home environment and sharing it with new people. Having personal space and privacy is important. Let children bring their own things and

---

Children will need time to adjust to new homes and circumstances, the ways that things are now done and sharing a parent's time

---

have at least a corner, or a cupboard, which is theirs. Talk about the need for privacy for all family members – you too!

The rewards

Although family change may be difficult, some children say that they can recognise improvements for them and their parents. Often seeing their parents happy in new relationships makes them feel that, although hard, sometimes family change is for the best.

• A big thank you to all the young people who contributed from: Camden Young Women's Centre, Calthorpe Project, Children's Express London Bureau, Hampden Youth Group, Ingestre Road Community Youth Programme, Making Links Peer Education Group Bangor, Townsend Church of England School, Venue Youth Club, The Lair Youth Project, The Northside Project Belfast, Plot Ten Community Play Project.

• If you would like further help and someone to talk to Call Parentline: 0808 800 2222. Textphone 0800 783 6783. 520 Highgate Studios, 53-79 Highgate Road, Kentish Town, London NW5 1TL. Tel: 020 7284 5500. www.parentlineplus.org.uk

Parentline Plus is the trading name of familylives.

© Parentline Plus

Net blamed for marital breakups

The Internet is becoming a frequent cause of the collapse of relationships, a leading marriage guidance organisation has warned. One in 10 of the 90,000 couples who seek the help of UK-based Relate now cite the Internet as a problem, with obsessive use of the medium blamed as well as its ability as a communication tool.

Both men and women complain of becoming Internet 'widows' as their partners spend hours at the computer downloading software or looking at pornography.

Sex chatlines and sites such as friendsreunited.co.uk, which can rekindle old school passions, pose further threats to relationships.

Relate's chief executive Angela Sibson told *The Times* newspaper: 'Our counsellors report that, more and more, the Internet is a relationship breaker.'

People aged between 25 and 35 were most vulnerable because they were the most frequent users of the Internet, Sibson's deputy Stephen Bagnall added.

'This is a peak time for people's first serious relationship to break up and it is also the age when many people get married for the first time,' he told the paper.

• The above information is an extract from Divorce-Online News, April 2002, from the web site www.divorce-online.co.uk

© Divorce-Online Limited

Not in front of the children

Increasing numbers of children experience the separation of their parents and life in stepfamilies. How do children view living in different kinds of families and what do they find helpful in working through these sometimes complex changes? Lorna Duckworth reports on work investigating the children's perspectives

The parents of nearly 150,000 British children get divorced each year. Many more youngsters watch their parents split up, knowing that family life will never be the same again. Although marital breakdown is increasingly common, a recent study shows that parents give their children very little explanation or chance to prepare for the upheaval. One parent is about to move out of the family home, a new partner appears on the scene, and the children suddenly have to divide their lives between two households.

Amid this turmoil, children are given very limited information about what is going on, according to research by Professor Judy Dunn and Kirby Deater-Deckard from King's College, London. Alarmingly, one in four children said no one talked to them about what was happening at the time of their parents' separation. Just five per cent of youngsters said they were given full explanations and the chance to ask questions.

Take, for example the sadness and confusion felt by this 10-year-old: 'I can't remember the very day, but I can remember a couple of weeks later when he came to visit me and I didn't know where he had gone or anything. So he kept on visiting me and he kept on driving off in the car. I had this rocking-horse by the window when I was little, and I used to sit up on the rocking-horse and watch his car into the distance. I used to cry my eyes out all night and most of the day. I'd cry and cry and cry.'

At a time when they are likely to be feeling anger, sadness and guilt themselves, communication is unlikely to be easy

---

By the age of 16, one in eight children in Britain will have experienced the separation of their parents and will be living with a step-parent as a result of remarriage or cohabitation. Children can be very resilient and most of them adapt to different family structures, maintaining good relationships with both parents, even when they live apart.

But not all youngsters cope well with family breakdown. Previous research by Rodgers and Prior, shows that the children of separated parents are twice as likely to display behavioural or emotional problems, or have difficulties at school (*Divorce and separation: The outcomes for children*, YPS, 1998). The report by Dunn and Deater-Deckard reinforces that message.

While the authors draw few conclusions, the study suggests that children cope better if they are consulted and have the chance to express their feelings. Those who are left in the dark may feel they are no longer loved by an absent parent or have problems adjusting to their 'divided' lives. It follows that the way parents handle their separation can have a big impact. At a time when they are likely to be feeling anger, sadness and guilt themselves, communication is unlikely to be easy. But all too often, it seems that parents do not know what to say to their children and are unable to offer reassurance or encourage their offspring to talk.

Professor Dunn's team interviewed 467 children between the

ages of five and 16 to find out what youngsters have to say about these experiences. The study included 248 youngsters living in stepfamilies, 106 living with single mothers and 113 living with both biological parents. Most of the children said they were confused and distressed by the separation. A quarter said no one talked to them when the break-up happened and just 17 per cent heard the news from their mother and father together. Nearly half of the children said they were given blunt statements, such as 'Daddy's leaving', while one in three were given some reasons, but no details and no chance to ask questions.

Grandparents and friends were the main confidants in the weeks after the separation, followed by birth mothers. In general, children were less likely to confide in fathers, stepfathers or other siblings. Children who were close to their maternal grandmothers had fewer adjustment problems such as anxiety, aggression or difficulties at school. These problems were more common among children who had troubled relationships with their parents, or if their own parents had encountered adversities such as a teenage pregnancy or a string of unsatisfactory relationships in their earlier lives. Many children missed their non-resident parent, which more often than not was their father, and longed to see them more. But more than half of the children who lived in two households, were positive about their twin existence. Those who were included in decisions about their living arrangements were happier than those who were unable to talk about moving between two homes.

Similar findings emerged from a recent Cardiff University study, in which 104 children aged between seven and 15, whose parents had recently divorced, were asked to talk about their feelings. Children spoke of their parents' separation as a 'crisis' in their lives about which they felt 'shock, disbelief and emotional distress'. Few children felt they were adequately prepared by their parents, even where the adults had been planning the split. When explanations were offered, children often said that the information was limited

and parents seldom discussed the emotional consequences of the experiences.

This differed from the recollection of parents, 99 per cent of whom said they had told the children about the divorces. But in reality, it appeared that half the parents had spoken to their children in any detail. Damien, aged 13, told the researchers. 'Mum just explained it to me, "Me and your Dad are getting divorced, we don't love each other any more", something like that. Just told me what it was.'

Both parents and children said they shied away from talking about divorce to protect the others' feelings. Six out of 10 children also decided to keep the divorce a secret from some people, with one boy relating how he had been called 'dad-less' by a friend. But both adults and children said they would have welcomed advice on how to deal with this stressful period of life.

In an attempt to minimise the damage inflicted by divorce, the Lord Chancellor's Department will next year test a proposal to establish Family Advice and Information Networks. Solicitor firms in six areas, together with voluntary organisations, will run 'pre-pilot' schemes offering marriage counselling, mediation, and help in talking to children. This is a start. But five years after the passage of the controversial Family Law Act 1996, progress towards providing better support for parents and overcoming the gap in communication seems remarkably slow.

The Cardiff academics, led by Professor Gillian Douglas, warned that help must be available to families at an early stage, and not simply when the legal system is invoked. After all, the initial separation may occur months, if not years, before parents 'finally resort to the legal system' to tidy up a divorce. They concluded: 'If parents are unable to provide the support children need, because of their own emotional difficulties and inability to communicate, it may be a matter of chance whether children find a suitable channel for their fears and feelings. Some are only left with "talking to teddy" when things get too much for them.

'It might be thought that a society concerned for the well-being of children should be doing much more to provide a rather more reliable form of support than this.'

● *Children's views of their changing families*, by Judy Dunn and Kirby Deater-Deckard, is published by YPS as part of the Foundation's Family Change series. It is available from York Publishing Services Ltd, 64 Hallfield Road, Layerthorpe, York, YO31 7ZQ. Tel: 01904 430033, Fax: 01904 430868, e-mail: orders@yps.ymn.co.uk (ISBN 1 84263 031 8, price £10.95).

● The above information is an extract from *Search 36*, Winter 2001/02, produced by the Joseph Rowntree Foundation.

© Joseph Rowntree Foundation

Give yourself a break

Staying together for the sake of the kids can be bad for you and for them. Miranda McMinn should know, she was six when her parents divorced

By Miranda McMinn

If you spent your twenties going to weddings every weekend to witness all your friends getting married, chances are that you spent your thirties observing many of the same people splitting up. Given that Britain has one of the highest divorce rates in Europe, this is hardly surprising. What is startling is the extent to which, in the run-up to the inevitable, so many people in miserable relationships buy the conservative line: 'We must stay together for the sake of the children.'

According to the *Daily Mail*'s Lynda Lee Potter, 'If [women] have children, they should grit their teeth and stick it out – even if their husband is tricky, a bore or a pain.'

I have a friend whose husband is all three of these things at once, yet she says to me sometimes, between sobs: 'I don't want my kids to come from a divorced home.' But why, I want to scream? Where's the guilt in finding a bit of happiness for yourself? And isn't it true that a happy parent equals a happy child?

I was six when my parents divorced. I remember their solemn faces and reassurances that 'We still love you, darling, it's just that we don't love each other any more.' Then my mum said that she and I were going to stay with friends who I knew had bunk beds. My response to the earth-shattering news was to ask if I'd get the top bunk. Of course there were repercussions – chiefly for my mother, who faced the difficult life of a single parent. But, to put it bluntly, it didn't do me any harm. I did sometimes wish they'd get back together, but this was for the sake of convention – I was the only child of divorced parents in my class and was as conformist as any primary-school child then or since.

Even as a child, when my mum explained that she and my father had separated because they didn't want me to grow up in an atmosphere where they were arguing all the time, I believed her. Research now backs this up. Professor E. Mavis Hetherington, author of *For Better or for Worse: Divorce Reconsidered*, studied 1,400 families, some over three decades. 'After 40 years of research,' she says, 'I harbour no doubts about the ability of divorce to devastate. It can and does ruin lives. I've seen it happen more times than I like to think about. But, that said, I also think much current writing on divorce has exaggerated its negative effects and ignored its sometimes considerable positive effects.' Her findings back up the commonsense view that if a marriage is unhappy, all those concerned may be better off out than in.

> **'I harbour no doubts about the ability of divorce to devastate. It can and does ruin lives. I've seen it happen more times than I like to think about'**

The reason I knew it made sense when my mum explained things was because I was happy. Friends still tell

me how jealous they were of me and my mum's cosy life together, tootling around town in our little car, or staying at home in our little flat, eating our supper off our knees in front of Mike Yarwood.

And consider the alternative. Stella, 33, a designer, reveals to me what might have been when she describes her own parents' unhappy marriage. 'I remember a palpable unhappiness. There was no rowing, just a kind of heavy feeling. When I look back, I think of this overhanging misery.

'There was a lot of crying in mum's bedroom with the door shut. In the evening we'd wait for him to come home after we'd had our tea and when he did the atmosphere would change – we were all on edge. Later on, my sister developed panic attacks and I suffered from anxiety.'

So, would things have been better if her parents had divorced? 'Yes, I probably do think that,' says Stella. 'From my point of view it would have lifted an atmosphere that was horribly tense. I could sense my dad's unhappiness, I could almost touch it. To have removed that would have made a big difference to me, my sister and my mum.'

So, why didn't they? Practical reasons, says Stella – her mother had never had a career and wouldn't have felt able to support her children – and because divorce wasn't an option in her family circle. 'But there was also that emotional stoicism. I really don't know what the value is in that. If they did it for my sake then it really is too ghastly to contemplate.'

Yet I'm the one who's supposed to be screwed up – because I'm the one who came from a broken home.

I ring my mum and quiz her on the events of 24 July 1972 – the day she left. 'People did think I should have stayed because of you,' she says. 'They became very smug about their own families and talked to my face about people who were very clever academically, but couldn't hold a family together – meaning me.

'I didn't think of divorce as a terrible black mark, I just thought of it as a release into a more positive world. But I don't think I ever slagged off your father to you – and that was a conscious thing.' Her method worked. I now have an enjoyable friendship with my dad.

Certainly it seems that if a marriage break-up is unavoidable, communication and positivity are vital assets. Research has shown that when children are invited to join in discussions about family life post-divorce, they are much more likely to take a positive view of events – yet in one study a quarter of the children interviewed said that at the time of their parents' separation no one had talked to them, and only five per cent had felt free to ask questions.

Louise, a 35-year-old solicitor whose parents divorced when she was six, agrees. 'My parents made every effort to be friends and to be positive to us. Initially it was a huge shock and I didn't handle it well.

'I refused to eat and they thought I had an eating disorder. But they behaved in a way that made it positive in the end. We acclimatised and grew up accepting the divorce.'

'I didn't think of divorce as a terrible black mark, I just thought of it as a release into a more positive world'

Natasha, 35, a writer whose relationship with her partner ended when their daughter was two-and-a-half, is one of a new generation looking beyond the cliché of the broken home. 'I didn't feel it was healthy to bring up a child in a situation where the parents were so hostile to each other,' she says. 'Now, regardless of what went on between us, her father and I are united in wanting her to be happy and as untraumatised by the experience as possible. We make sure that we do things together, all three of us, like going for a meal or to the cinema. Children are very of the moment so she's got no concept of what it could be like – unless friends started saying to her "You haven't got a daddy", and people just don't do that any more.'

If all the propaganda were to be believed, people like me should now be on the scrap heap – depressed, anxious alcoholics or drug addicts who can't sustain relationships or hold down jobs. In fact, I'm happily married with a daughter. If my husband and I were to divorce, I'd be heartbroken. But the heartbreak would be for my own sake – not for the sake of the children.

• This article first appeared in *The Observer*, 21 April 2002.

© Guardian Newspapers Limited 2002

Divorce rates fall to their lowest level in 20 years

By Nicole Martin

The number of people getting divorced has fallen to its lowest level in more than 20 years, according to the latest government figures.

There were 141,135 divorces in England and Wales last year, compared with 144,556 in 1999 and 138,706 in 1979, the Office for National Statistics said.

At the same time, the divorce rate per 1,000 of the married population dropped to its lowest since 1984. Last year 12.7 people in every 1,000 of those married got a divorce, compared with 13 in 1999. It was 12 in 1984 and 11.2 in 1979.

Experts yesterday attributed the fall to a decline in marriage and the growing popularity of cohabitation, as well as to greater efforts by couples to salvage their relationships.

Figures published last year showed that the number of couples getting married had fallen by around a quarter over 10 years.

There were 263,515 marriages in England and Wales in 1999, the latest year for which data is available, compared with 346,697 in 1989 and 368,853 in 1979.

Robert Whelan, director of Family and Youth Concern, said it would be wrong to welcome the figures.

He said: 'We think, "Good, divorce is down", when we see this, but the proportion of the population that is married is down.

There were 141,135 divorces in England and Wales last year, compared with 144,556 in 1999 and 138,706 in 1979

'Cohabitation is increasingly an alternative to marriage rather than preparation for it. We find this very worrying because for us marriage offers the best environment to bring up children.'

But Denise Knowles, of the marriage guidance group Relate, said it was too simplistic to blame a drop in the number of marriages. She said a growing number of couples were fighting to save their marriages.

She said: 'The other factors we have to look at here are that people are marrying later in life so perhaps are more aware of what they want from marriage.

'People are also now of a generation that has seen the effects of parents and friends getting a divorce. They know how it can affect children and so think more carefully about the relationship before turning to divorce.'

© Telegraph Group Limited, London 2002

ADDITIONAL RESOURCES

You might like to contact the following organisations for further information. Due to the increasing cost of postage, many organisations cannot respond to enquiries unless they receive a stamped, addressed envelope.

CARE (Christian Action Research and Education)
53 Romney Street
London, SW1P 3RF
Tel: 020 7233 0455
Fax: 020 7233 0983
E-mail: info@care.org.uk
Web site: www.care.org.uk
A Christian charity which produces a wide range of publications presenting a Christian perspective on moral issues.

Centre for Policy Studies (CPS)
57 Tufton Street
London, SW1P 3QL
Tel: 020 7222 4488
Fax: 020 7222 4388
Web site: www.cps.org.uk
CPS is an independent centre-right think tank which develops and publishes public policy proposals and arranges seminars and lectures on topical policy issues, as part of its mission to influence policy around the world.

ChildLine
2nd Floor Royal Mail Building
50 Studd Street
London, N1 0QW
Tel: 020 7239 1000
Fax: 020 7239 1001
E-mail: reception@childline.org.uk
Web site: www.childline.org.uk
ChildLine is a free, national helpline for children and young people in trouble or danger. Provides confidential phone counselling service for any child with any problem 24 hours a day. Produces publications. Children or young people can phone or write free of charge about problems of any kind to: ChildLine, Freepost 1111, London N1 0BR, Tel: Freephone 0800 1111.

Family Matters Institute (FMI)
The Park, Moggerhanger
Bedfordshire, MK44 3RW
Tel: 01767 641002
Fax: 01767 641515
E-mail: family@familymatters.org.uk
Web site: www.familymatters.org.uk

Family Matters Institute's purpose is to work alongside church, faith and community leaders to support and strengthen marriage, parenting and all aspects of family life.

National Children's Bureau (NCB)
8 Wakley Street
London, EC1V 7QE
Tel: 020 7843 6000
Fax: 020 7843 9512
Web site: www.ncb.org.uk
The National Children's Bureau promotes the interests and well-being of all children and young people across every aspect of their lives.

National Family and Parenting Institute (NFPI)
430 Highgate Studios
58-79 Highgate Road
London, NW5 1TL
Tel: 020 7424 3460
Fax: 020 7424 3590
E-mail: info@nfpi.org
Web site: www.nfpi.org and www.e-parents.org
An independent charity working to improve the lives of parents and families by campaigning for a more family-friendly society.

National Family Mediation (NFM)
Star House, 104-108 Grafton Road
London, NW5 4BD
Tel: 0207 485 9066
Fax: 0207 284 1881
E-mail: general@nfm.org.uk
Web site: www.nfm.u-net.com/
National Family Mediation is a network of over 60 local not-for-profit Family Mediation Services in England and Wales offering help to couples, married or unmarried, who are in the process of separation and divorce.

National Youth Agency (NYA)
17-23 Albion Street
Leicester, LE1 6GD
Tel: 0116 285 3700
Fax: 0116 285 3777
E-mail: nya@nya.org.uk
Web site: www.nya.org.uk and www.youthinformation.com

The National Youth Agency aims to advance youth work to promote young people's personal and social development, and their voice, influence and place in society. Produces the publication *Young People Now*.

NCH
85 Highbury Park
London, N5 1UD
Tel: 020 7704 7000
Fax: 020 7226 2537
Web site: www.nch.org.uk
NCH improves the lives of Britain's most vulnerable children and young people by providing a diverse and innovative range of services for them and their families and campaigning on their behalf.

One Plus One Marriage and Partnership Research
14 Theobalds Road
London, WC1X 8PF
Tel: 020 7841 3660
Fax: 020 7831 5263
Web site: www.oneplusone.org.uk
One Plus One is an independent research organisation whose role is to generate knowledge about marriage and relationships – how they work, why they can sometimes run into difficulties and how couples cope when they do.

Parentline Plus
Unit 520 Highgate Studios
53-57 Highgate Road
London, NW5 1TL
Tel: 020 7284 5500
Fax: 020 7284 5501
E-mail: centraloffice@parentlineplus.org.uk
Web site: www.parentlineplus.org.uk
A national helpline for parents under stress. Parentline is the national freephone helpline run by Parentline Plus. Contact Parentline on 0808 800 2222 Monday-Friday 9am-9pm, Saturdays 9.30am-5pm and Sundays from 10am-3pm.
Text phone: 0800 783 6783.

INDEX

ACKNOWLEDGEMENTS

The publisher is grateful for permission to reproduce the following material.

While every care has been taken to trace and acknowledge copyright, the publisher tenders its apology for any accidental infringement or where copyright has proved untraceable. The publisher would be pleased to come to a suitable arrangement in any such case with the rightful owner.

Chapter One: Marriage and Cohabitation

The family today, © National Family and Parenting Institute (NFPI), *Changing trends in family life*, © CARE – Christian Action Research and Education, *Marriages and divorces in the UK*, © Crown copyright is reproduced with the permission of the Controller of Her Majesty's Stationery Office, *Proportion of the population by marital status and gender*, © Crown copyright is reproduced with the permission of the Controller of Her Majesty's Stationery Office, *Marriages up for the first time in eight years*, © Telegraph Group Limited, London 2002, *Marriage – raising questions, finding answers*, © One Plus One Marriage and Partnership Research, *First marriages*, © Crown copyright is reproduced with the permission of the Controller of Her Majesty's Stationery Office, *Young people's views*, © The National Children's Bureau (NCB), *Marriage expectations*, © Crown copyright is reproduced with the permission of the Controller of Her Majesty's Stationery Office, *Live-in partners find love doesn't last*, © The Daily Mail, January 2002, *Get hitched for health and happiness*, © CARE – Christian Action Research and Education, *The truth about marriage*, © MORI (Market & Opinion Research International Limited), *Children pay the price when their parents don't marry*, © Telegraph Group Limited, London 2002, *Marriages make a millennium comeback*, © Telegraph Group Limited, London 2002, *Marriage and living together*, © 2002 National Youth Agency, *Death of marriage*, © The Daily Mail, April 2002, *Number of marriages, England and Wales*, © Crown copyright is reproduced with the permission of the Controller of Her Majesty's Stationery Office, *Marriage is for love, not life*, © Guardian Newspapers Limited 2002, *Loosening the knot*, © Guardian Newspapers Limited 2002, *I do, I do, I do, I do . . .*, © Guardian Newspapers Limited 2002, *Second-timers are bringing marriage back into fashion*, © The Daily Mail, March 2002, *It can be arranged*, © Exposure Magazine, *Court annuls arranged marriage*, © Guardian Newspapers Limited 2002.

Chapter Two: Separation and Divorce

Divorce and separation, © 2002 National Youth Agency, *Broken hearts*, © Centre for Policy Studies, *Age at first marriage*, © Crown copyright is reproduced with the permission of the Controller of Her Majesty's Stationery Office, *The cost of family breakdown*, © Family Matters Institute, *Children and divorce*, © Divorce-Online Limited, *D-I-V-O-R-C-E*, © Guardian Newspapers Limited 2002, *Helping children cope with divorce*, © NCH, *My family's changing*, © Crown copyright is reproduced with the permission of the Controller of Her Majesty's Stationery Office, *Marriages and divorces*, © Crown copyright is reproduced with the permission of the Controller of Her Majesty's Stationery Office, *Family mediation*, © National Family Mediation (NFM), *Stepfamilies*, © ChildLine, *Divorce, separation, new families*, © Parentline Plus, *Net blamed for marital breakups*, © Divorce-Online Limited, *Not in front of the children*, © Joseph Rowntree Foundation, *Give yourself a break*, © Guardian Newspapers Limited 2002, *Divorce rates fall to their lowest level in 20 years*, © Telegraph Group Limited, London 2002.

Photographs and illustrations:

Pages 1, 11, 17, 25, 32, 35: Simon Kneebone; pages 6, 22, 29: Fiona Katauskas; pages 8, 28, 37: Bev Aisbett; pages 18, 26, 38: Pumpkin House.

Craig Donnellan
Cambridge
September, 2002